FIFTY CENTURIES OF ART

APHRODITE

Marble statue, perhaps by a Greek sculptor, made in the 1st century B.C. *after a Greek original of about 300* B.C. *This and the celebrated marble Medici Venus in Florence are from the same original, possibly a bronze by Praxiteles. There is some reason to believe that this statue was sold by Winkelmann in the 18th century to a German nobleman from whose heirs the Metropolitan acquired it.*

FIFTY CENTURIES OF ART

By

FRANCIS HENRY TAYLOR

Published for

THE METROPOLITAN MUSEUM OF ART

by

HARPER & BROTHERS, NEW YORK

For the Two Pamelas, Emily, Molly and John

Acknowledgments

Except where otherwise noted the illustrations and reproductions in this book are from the collections of The Metropolitan Museum of Art. Special acknowledgments are made to the following individuals and institutions, who have permitted the reproduction of illustrations indicated in the captions: Mr. Chester Dale, Mrs. David M. Giltinan, Mr. Edward Hopper, Mr. Robert Lehman, Mr. Duncan Phillips, Mr. Richard D. Tucker, Mr. Carroll S. Tyson, Mr. Vincent W. Van Gogh; The Academy, Florence; The Art Institute of Chicago; The Church of San Pietro in Vincoli, Rome; The Church of Santa Maria delle Grazie, Milan; Detroit Institute of Fine Arts; Doria Gallery, Rome; Huntington Library, San Marino, California; Jan Six Museum, Amsterdam; Kaiser Friedrich Museum, Berlin; Kunsthistorisches Museum, Vienna; The Louvre, Paris; Mauritshuis, The Hague; Minneapolis Institute of Arts; Municipal Museum, Amsterdam; Musée Granet, Aix-en-Provence; Museo Civico di Padova; Museum of Fine Arts, Boston; Museum of Modern Art, New York; The National Gallery, London; The National Gallery of Art, Washington; New York State Historical Society; Opera Medicea Laurenziana, Florence; Philadelphia Museum of Art; Pierpont Morgan Library, New York; The Prado Museum, Madrid; Rijksmuseum, Amsterdam; Commune di Borgo San Sepolcro; Tate Gallery, London; Uffizi Gallery, Florence.

To Art Color Slides, Inc., New York; Art News, New York; Artext Publishing Co., Westport, Conn.; Roberto Hoesch, Milan; the editors of *Life*, New York; Hans Prell, Amsterdam; and Éditions d'Art, Albert Skira, F. A., Geneva, are due especial thanks for photographic permissions granted by them, as well as to the Book-of-the-Month Club, Inc., publishers and distributors of the *Metropolitan Museum of Art Miniatures*.

The author further wishes to acknowledge the constant and invaluable assistance given by the Editorial Department of The Metropolitan Museum of Art, and by the members of the Museum Staff, and by other authors who have contributed to the texts of the *Metropolitan Museum of Art Miniatures*. The albums prepared by Sidney Freedberg, A. Hyatt Mayor, George Sarton and Margaret Scherer have been particularly helpful. He also wishes to acknowledge his indebtedness to a *Handbook to the Collections of the Worcester Art Museum*, edition of 1933, and to a catalogue of *An Exhibition of the Art of the Dark Ages*, also published by the Worcester Art Museum, in 1937, of both of which he was author and editor.

Foreword

FOR the past five years the Metropolitan Museum has been publishing and distributing through the Book-of-the-Month Club, Inc., a series of albums containing sheets of twenty-four illustrations in full color of many of the world's great masterpieces. Approximately five millions of these albums, each accompanied with appropriate text, have been distributed throughout the United States and Canada. This unexpected and overwhelming response, particularly in rural communities and on the part of those who do not have regular access to the treasures of the larger cities, has broadened the Museum's responsibilities to this large audience. Thousands of inquiries have been received asking whether it might not be possible for the Museum to make available in more permanent form the fruits of this enormous investment in color photography and engraving. In addition to this body of color plates, amounting in all to over a thousand subjects, the Museum also controls a very substantial group of larger plates in varying sizes which have accumulated as a by-product of the Museum's educational publications.

To meet these requests the Chairman of Harper & Brothers, Cass Canfield, with the cooperation of the Trustees of the Museum and of the officers of the Book-of-the-Month Club, Inc., commissioned the author to prepare a brief outline of the history of art utilizing as many as possible of the existing color plates. These reproductions, together with about a dozen obtained from outside sources, give a very wide coverage of great paintings, sculptures and objects of art throughout the ages. About two-thirds are reproductions from the vast collection in the Metropolitan; one-third represents objects from famous museums in other cities, such as the Louvre, the National Galleries in Washington and London, the Prado.

Thus *Fifty Centuries of Art* is presented to the public as the first general survey of art ever to be published in full color. And it is available at a price nearly everyone can afford. Containing 342 illustrations, it is addressed not only to students in high schools and in the colleges but it is intended for that great multitude who claim to know nothing about art but "know what they like." Some sixty million of the latter throng our art galleries and museums each year. Now that color television has at last become a reality, the broadcasting of art exhibitions into their homes is fast becoming a daily occurrence. For them this book can be a constant companion and source of ready reference, both at home and on their travels abroad—a curtain raiser to the sumptuous, never-ending pageant of human civilization.

F. H. T.

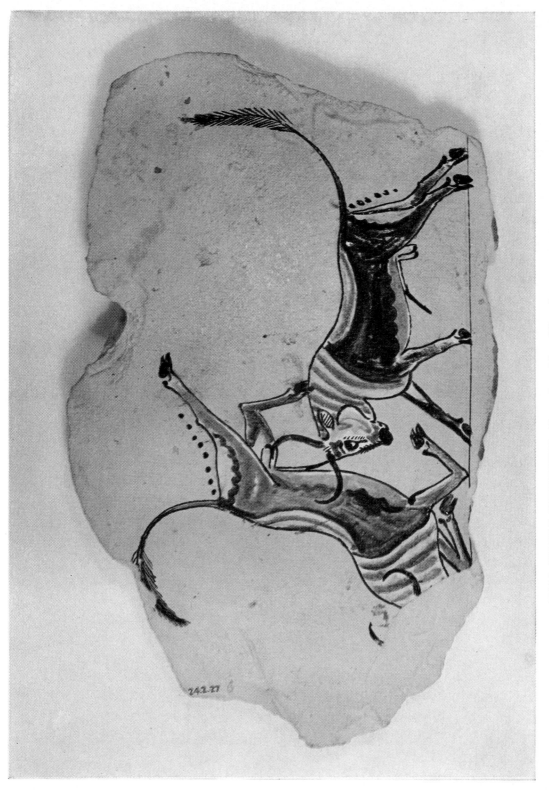

TWO BULLS FIGHTING. Egyptian, New Kingdom, 1567–1085 B.C.

This fragment of ancient painting follows a tradition of animal drawing that goes very far back in prehistoric times to the cave paintings at Altamira in Spain and forms a link with the late Cretan paintings of bulls (2000–1750 B.C.) discovered in the palace of King Minos at Cnossos.

Egypt and the Ancient East

THE birth of Western civilization took place in the lower Mediterranean basin along the Valley of the Nile, and in the sandy, arid plains of Mesopotamia extending between the Tigris and Euphrates rivers.

Emerging from the chaos of prehistory with the builders of the Pyramids, about 3000 B.C., Egyptian art flourished in four great periods: the Old, or Memphite Kingdom (2780–2280 B.C.), the Middle Kingdom (2134–1778 B.C.), the New or Theban Kingdom (1567–1085 B.C.), and the later Saitic and Ptolemaic periods that terminated in Roman times. The two principal characteristics of this art are its monumental majesty and its concern with death and the life hereafter. The gigantic temples and rock-cut tombs of Memphis and Luxor, like the man-made pyramids of Gizeh, are imbued not only with an overpowering sense of mass and weight but are also the solemn witnesses of the Egyptian's religious superstition. In the belief that every individual is possessed of a double or *Ka* who never leaves him even at death, the body of the deceased was mummified to insure its lasting preservation, and with it in the tomb were placed objects of daily use which the dead person might require in the world beyond. Sealed supposedly forever from human view, and exposed only in recent years by the curiosity of archaeologists, these objects have retained in the mild, dry air of Egypt a freshness of color and a perfection of preservation virtually unparalleled in any other art.

Because the Pharaohs were themselves divinities, the palaces of the living shared the hieratic splendor and formality of the temples and tomb chambers. Preceded usually by colossal *pylons*, or entrance gates, the forecourts opened on forests of colonnades and heroic statues of the local gods; on either side were the living and ceremonial quarters of the palace, while to the rear, hidden from the gaze of the vulgar, was the sanctuary of the reigning god. The walls and columns of halls and peristyles were covered with painted low reliefs, an art in which the Egyptians excelled, and brilliant decorations of glazed brick and colored glass.

Sculpture, painting and the decorative arts of the household followed closely the spirit and patterns of Egyptian architecture. They were not occupied with modern theories of perspective; their representations were flat and two-dimensional, objects in the background being placed in horizontal bands above the principal figures of the composition. A rigid frontality dominated their figures of human beings; little attempt was made at likeness or portraiture; the use of geometric designs and severe stylizations of natural phenomena enhanced by violently contrasting colors, produced a

LOTIFORM CUP, Faïence
XIX–XX Dynasty, 1320–1085 B.C.

FISHING AND FOWLING SKIFF, Painted Wood
Theban tomb model, XI Dynasty, c. 2000 B.C.

This ship model is characteristic of the ship models which have recently been discovered in the tomb chambers of the great Pyramid at Gizeh.

definition of form and, purity of line dramatized in the blazing sunlight of North Africa.

The art of Mesopotamia, influenced successively by the civilizations of Chaldea, Assyria, Babylonia and Persia, derived its essential character from the art of the Nile Valley. Each of these ancient peoples in turn built tremendous palaces from which arose high towers, or Ziggurats, of which the Tower of Babel was a legendary example. Lined with galleries of vivid glazed brick and alabaster relief, their palaces were sumptuous beyond description, and the splendor of their terraces was such that the "hanging gardens of Babylon" have ever since been a byword for the sybaritic and the prodigal. Sculptures from the palaces of Khorsabad and Persepolis, Nineveh and Calah now in the great museums of Paris, London and New York, and dedicated to the narration of scenes of military combat and the chase, already begin to show a freedom from the conventions of the Egyptians. No more brilliant chapter in the

SHAWABTY FIGURES, c. 1400 B.C.

history of archaeology has been written than that devoted to the new discoveries in these cultures during the past fifty years. Now much that was long accepted as poetic allegory of the Old Testament has been substantiated. The world of Moses, of Sennacherib, of Sargon "the law giver," and of Darius and Xerxes has come alive.

RAMESES II, 1290–1280 B.C.

TWO MEN AND A BOY, c. 1360 B.C.

EGYPTIAN ART

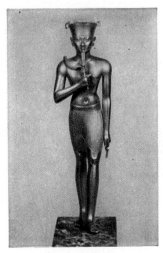

AMUN, c. 1450 b.c.

MUSICIANS, ENCAUSTIC, 1400 b.c.

HIEROGLYPH, 500–330 b.c.

BRONZE CAT, c. 300 b.c.

EGYPTIAN ART

WINGED BULL, 885–860 B.C., Assyrian

The Art of Greece and Rome

THE civilization which flourished on the mainland of Greece, and which ultimately dominated the entire lower basin of the Mediterranean Sea (Italy, Sicily, Asia Minor, the Greek Islands and North Africa), is the basis of the world in which we live today. The Greek ideals of beauty, of balance and of logic have become our ideals. The Greeks were the first to grasp the facts and implications of the material world and to relate themselves to it. Clarity of vision and expression, and the ability to isolate an idea from its background and generalize it, were the qualities which permitted the Greek artist to depart from the earlier conventions of the Egyptians and Assyrians and to represent abstract rational ideas. There is ever present in Greek art a unity of concept, a harmony of the masses, a finish of detail and distinction to the whole which governs every work of architecture, sculpture and painting.

The Homeric poems depict the gradual merging of the cultures of the rough Doric mountaineers who descended upon the Mycenaeans about 1100 B.C. with those of the seafaring tribes of Ionia in Asia Minor and the Greek Islands. For a thousand years the art forms of Egypt and Mesopotamia had been filtering in by way of Crete. Little by little, beginning with the sixth century B.C., the stiff frontality of archaic sculpture gave way to the Hellenic desire to glorify the human body and to permit that freer interpretation of nature and of movement so evident in their love of athletics and the Olympic Games.

FIFTY CENTURIES OF ART

NIKÉ AND A VICTOR, Terracotta Bobbin
Attributed to the Penthesilea Painter, Attic, 460–450 B.C.

ATHENA C. 460 B.C.

The classic period of Greek sculpture in Athens was the Age of Pericles in the fifth century when the Temple of Athena, the Parthenon, destroyed by the Persians, was rebuilt. Its sculpture was the work of Phidias and his pupils. The "Olympian calm," the almost superhuman beauty of his figures, has since remained the ideal of the classical point of view. The little bronze of *Athena with Her Owl* shown above, from the collection of the same Lord Elgin who brought the marbles of the Parthenon to London, closely approaches the style of Phidias. Toward the end of the fifth century, and throughout the fourth, the marble cutters of Athens yielded more and more to the seductions of naturalism. A new grace and intimacy were evident in the works of the three great sculptors: Scopas, Lysippus and Praxiteles (cf. frontispiece). During the third century B.C. the armies of Alexander the Great carried the Hellenic or Greek civilization of the mainland to the cities of Pergamum and Antioch in Asia Minor and to Alexandria in Egypt. There the natural poise and calm of Greek art were replaced by the frenzied realism and overdecoration of the so-called Hellenistic style.

STATUETTE OF HORSE. 5TH CENT. B.C.

GEOMETRIC HORSE. 8TH CENT. B.C.

GREEK ART

THE "LANSDOWNE" AMAZON

*Like the athlete's head below, this a Roman copy
of a Greek 5th century original attributed to the
workshops of Phidias, Polyclitus and Kresilas.*

Simultaneously with the spread of Greek colonies to Sicily and Lower Italy the
rise of the Latin Republic with its absorption of the native cultures of the Villanovans
and Etruscans was giving form and substance to Roman art. As opposed to the Greeks
who were contemplative and thought in abstract terms, the Romans were men of
practical affairs, governed by an interest in the immediate and the actual. Therefore,
Roman architecture, though less perfect and subtle in its proportions than the Greek,
far surpassed the latter in practical invention and engineering; mastering the principle
of the arch, the Romans were able to build on a gigantic scale and thus lay the foundations of the familiar "classic style" of modern architecture. Roman sculpture, lacking
the refinements and ideals of Greek beauty, excelled in portraiture.

ETRUSCAN WARRIOR, 500 B.C.

DIADOUMENOS.

GRAECO-ROMAN ART

RED-FIGURED CUP

The monumental painting of Greece has mostly vanished with the course of time. During the archaic and classic periods nearly all the works of sculpture were painted, although today only the merest traces of coloring remain. Our knowledge of Greek painting is thus derived from the incomparable art of the potter and vase painter, perhaps the most perfect expression of the Hellenic genius. Divided into certain families or groups according to their ceremonial uses, the flawless beauty and homogeneity of these "Attic shapes" have never been surpassed. The earliest were the archaic or Proto-Corinthian vases simply decorated on a yellow ground with geometric and stylized animal forms, similar to the ceramics of Crete and Mycenae. In the sixth century a Black-figured Style was adopted by the Athenians in which the designs were painted in black on red clay. A hundred years later the reverse of this process resulted in the Red-figured Style; funerary vases, or *lekythoi*, and certain other ceramic types, show designs and figures drawn on a white ground.

PAINTING A STATUE

BLACK-FIGURED JAR

GREEK VASE PAINTING (500–300 B.C.)

GEOMETRIC JAR, Archaic

HELLENISTIC BRONZE

TOILET BOX, Terracotta
465–460 B.C.

MOSAIC, 1ST CENT. B.C. – 1ST CENT. A.D.

HERMARCHOS, 3RD CENT. B.C.

GREEK ART

MUMMY PORTRAIT
Fayoum, Egypt, 2ND CENT., A.D.

ROMAN MURAL

ROMAN MURAL
1ST CENT., B.C.

Roman painting developed from the monumental style of Greece. In frescoes from Pompeii and Boscoreale, and in mosaics recently unearthed in North Africa and Syria, we see for the first time in Western art an attempt to create the illusion of natural landscape, observing the usual three-dimensional relations of background to middle- and fore-ground. After the second century A.D. there arose in Europe two great traditions of painting—this Latin tradition emerging from Pompeii and Alexandria, and the opposing style of Byzantium, the capital of the Eastern Roman Empire. The latter, more formal and luxurious than Latin art, married the oriental love of brilliant color and repetitive accents of design with the ancient Greek gift for isolating figures in abstract neutral space. In Byzantine art background was merely an element of decoration; perspective and the relation of receding planes were utterly disregarded and the composition appears flat, the figures giving the impression of having been cut out and placed against a screen. The fusion of these currents, Latin and Byzantine, in the twelfth and thirteenth centuries became the chief preoccupation of the artists of Italy.

WOMAN PLAYING THE KITHERA, WITH HER SERVANT
Mural from the triclinium of a villa at Boscoreale near Pompeii, Roman, 1ST CENT., A.D.

GOLD GLASS

GOLD-GLASS PORTRAIT

"ANTIOCH CHALICE"

MARRIAGE SCENE (?)

SILVER DISH

LATE ROMAN AND BYZANTINE ART (3RD–6TH CENT. A.D.)

Art of the Far East

ALTHOUGH the origins of Chinese art are very obscure, it has had, perhaps, the longest continuous duration of any art the world has ever known, lasting unbroken from the third millennium B.C. to our own times. Early in the first century B.C. the Chinese had established contact with Parthians and Syrians in Northern Persia; six hundred years later they invaded Turkestan and India, and, by the time of Charlemagne, a Chinese emperor had conquered Chaldea and established a protectorate over Mesopotamia. Relations with Greece and Rome had earlier been effected through the campaigns of Alexander the Great and the Caesars. Later, in the thirteenth century, the Mongols invaded Arabia, and at the moment when the Pilgrim Fathers were settling in the Massachusetts Bay Colony, Burma and Indo-China were subjugated by the Chinese war lords. The art of China, without losing its own character and originality, accepted all these foreign influences and made them its own.

Just as the Christian story was to dominate the art of the West for a thousand years, the legend of Buddha Sakyamuni, a prince of Benares in India who in the sixth century B.C., like Saint Francis of Assisi, left his father's home and riches to live a life of solitude, was to become the central theme of the Oriental painter and sculptor. Since the Buddha, through asceticism and self-denial achieved Nirvana, the state of perfect blessedness, the ideal of Buddhist art was not physical beauty, as it was with the Greeks, but the expression of a divine grace and wisdom. Mysticism and contemplation, indicated by simplification of contour and attenuation of the figure took precedence over the realism of anatomical detail.

We have only the most fragmentary knowledge of the prehistoric civilizations of China. Magnificent ornaments in jade, sacrificial bronze vessels and carved ivories have come down to us. But not until the Han Dynasty (202 B.C.–220 A.D.) did a monumental art appear, of which majestic sculpture cut in stone in low relief, and archaic figures of men and animals survive. Pottery figurines of horses and musicians as well as funerary tiles were decorated profusely.

With the downfall of the Han Dynasty there followed a period of civil strife during which a new art developed and Buddhism was introduced from India. In the sculpture of the rock-cut temple caves at Yün Kang and Lung-men Chinese sculpture reached its apogee under the T'ang (A.D. 618–908). Naturalism replaced conventionality and the spiritual, idealized portrait took on the likeness of living persons.

BUDDHA FROM YÜN KANG

The later dynasties, Sung, Yüan and Ming (A.D. 960–1644) marked a relaxation of the more orthodox Buddhism in favor of the moral teachings of Confucius with the result that sculpture, which heretofore had exclusively served religion, in a great measure declined. Painting, on the other hand, rose to new heights. Exquisite palace scenes of classic ladies of the T'ang period are forsaken for the contemplation of nature. A Buddhist sect, the Zen, developed a school of landscape painting which sought not so much to depict the scene itself as it did to reveal its inward spirit, thus arousing an emotional response in the spectator. The appreciation of the subtleties of nature, which the Chinese and Japanese reflect in their art and poetry, far surpasses anything we know in the West. To the Chinese, landscape includes men and all living things. Man, whose nude body is the most significant and expressive motif of Western art, is here

GILT-BRONZE BUDDHA

KUAN YIN, Gilded Wood

CHINESE ART (5TH–13TH CENT. A.D.)

SPRING MORNING AT THE PALACES OF HAN
Detail from a handscroll painting on silk, Sung, 960–1280

merely incidental to the whole; flowers and animals are equally important. The life of action is subordinated to the life of contemplation.

Chinese painting is a form of calligraphy or handwriting practiced with a fine brush held vertically above the silk or specially prepared rice paper. Ink or bister is the favorite medium. The paintings are of two kinds—hanging pictures and horizontal hand scrolls, kept rolled up and shown on occasion. The handscrolls, opened bit by bit, permit the spectator to travel through the landscape in a way that is impossible in the more static, framed European canvas. Once the painter has touched his brush to the silk his stroke is final; he must work quickly, having his ideas and composition clearly defined in his own mind before he starts. There is an almost miniature precision to every stroke, every detail and the strict conventions of painting rocks, trees and mountains still persist. It has been called "boneless painting," that is to say, by gradations of monochrome it faintly suggests the outline of objects in successive planes.

HEAD FROM YÜN KANG
5TH CENT.

VASE, Tz'u Chou Ware

VASE, Ox-blood Glaze

BUDDHIST ALTARPIECE

VESSEL, BIRD COVER

EARLY CHINESE ART

THE LADY SU HUI AND ATTENDANTS

THE MOUNTAIN PINE

THE PLEASURE OF THE FISHES

JADE STAG

GLAZED POTTERY DOG

CHINESE ART (1000 B.C.–1644 A.D.)

FLOWERING MALLOW AND EGRET
Chao Meng-Chien (?) Sung Dynasty

The Sung Dynasty (960–1280) corresponded both in date and temper to the era of religious fervor in medieval Europe. The Yüan or Mongol period which followed (1280–1368), saw, as in fourteenth-century Italy, a return to the classical imitation of the old masters. On the other hand, in the Ming Dynasty (1368–1644), the moment of our Western Renaissance, the interior glow that had suffused the earlier art of China gradually fades away. Concentrated within herself, she ceased to have contact with the outer world and Chinese art became concerned rather with the beauty of material things than with the expression of the inner spirit. In fact, this was so much the case that during the Ch'ing and Manchu dynasties (1644–1911) painters and sculptors gradually yielded their place to the artisans in lacquer, porcelain and jade.

The art of Japan, so dependent on that of China for all its forms, reflects the great differences in temperament that exist between the two peoples. The calm, patient, philosophical discipline of the Chinese is replaced by an animation of spirit, a happiness of expression and a witty sense of narrative that is exquisite, brittle and refined.

FIFTY CENTURIES OF ART

POPPIES (Slightly Cropped), Probably by Sosetsu

The principal epochs of Japanese art are, first, the successive primitive periods lasting through the ninth century, during which reliance was wholly upon the Chinese. The style is solemn and majestic but rather dry in comparison with that of the mainland. Then from the tenth to the fourteenth century in the Fujiwara and Kamakura periods a purely native Japanese style of painting religious subjects on gold background was evolved. In the Ashikaga period (1333–1568) a renaissance of Japanese art took place establishing two clearly defined trends, the realistic and vivid Kano school, and the academic conservative tradition of the aristocracy in the Tosa school.

During the Tokugawa period (1615–1867) the academic and aristocratic tradition disappears and is replaced in the eighteenth century by a wave of popular realism. The great plebeian school of woodblock printing in color on paper was developed. These prints or "Miserable World Pictures," of which two are shown here, a *primitive* by Sharaku, and *Landscape in the Rain* by Hiroshige, had an enormous influence on the French Impressionist painters of the latter half of the nineteenth century.

TREE IN RAIN—HIROSHIGE

THE GREAT WAVE—HOKUSAI

JAPANESE ART

ICHIKAWA EBIZO IV–SHARAKU

GIRL WITH LANTERN
HARUNOBU

JAPANESE ART

The Art of Islam

FROM the death of the Prophet in A.D. 632 the religion of Mohammed spread east to Persia and India, west along both shores of the Mediterranean to Spain; and north through the Balkans and Central Europe as far as Vienna, where the Turks were finally stopped at the walls of the city in the seventeenth century. There are five separate and distinct schools of Islamic art: that of Syria and Egypt, the schools of Persia, Ottoman Turkey and Anatolia, India, the western schools of North Africa and Spain, and the Arabo-Norman school of Sicily. It is above all an art of decoration relying chiefly upon geometric and floral patterns, since the representation of human or animal figures was prohibited in religious art or architecture, although it was allowed in the embellishment of domestic articles and secular texts. For this reason Islamic artists became supreme masters of arabesque ornament and interlacing.

There is, to be exact, no essential native style, for the art of Islam took on the attributes and color of each new people subjugated by the faithful. Of all the schools that of Persia had the longest duration and was, perhaps, the purest and most original. Islam not only absorbed and attracted foreign ideas, but in turn influenced the peoples with whom it came in contact. Barbarian migrations from Scythia and South Russia and the conquests of Alexander the Great had much earlier tended to Hellenize the indigenous cultures of Iran and Mesopotamia.

Although there had been a gradual penetration of oriental ideas into Europe from Byzantium and along the trade and pilgrimage routes, the great impact of the East on Latin Christianity was not felt until the Crusades. The European knights were exposed not only to Arabian medicine and mathematics, they saw also the great vaulted cupolas, the mosques and early Christian churches which reflected the sumptuous palaces of the Sassanid kings. They likewise discovered the groined vault which was to enable the Gothic cathedral builders to overcome the limitations of the barrel vault which the Romanesque masons had carried over from the Roman basilica.

In Persia the art of the potter was developed to a very high degree. The earliest centers were at Nishapur, Rayy (Rhages) and Kashan. Gradually the primitive rough-fired pottery was superseded by green glaze and polychrome ware in which Mongol influence, particularly in their method of drawing faces, is evident. A brisk and constant trade carried on for many centuries over the camel caravan routes to China brought the art of the Near East closer to the extreme Orient than to Europe.

THE TURQUOISE PAVILION
Persian miniature painting, 16TH CENT.

Despite the invasions and constant warfare that ravaged the country from the ninth century to the sixteenth, when she at last regained her independence and prosperity under the Safavid dynasty, Persia continued to foster the arts. A rich tradition of metalwork and silk weaving had flourished without interruption from the time of the Sassanids; rug weaving reached its apogee about 1500. But it was in the writing and illuminating of manuscripts that her artists excelled. Whereas the Koran was never enriched with illustrations, it was ornamented with superb calligraphy, marginal medallions and title pages. At first non-representational, little by little the designs became more fluid and relaxed, imitating both in color and pattern the rugs of the same period. Secular manuscripts, particularly of epic and love poetry, were, however, illustrated with charming scenes and vignettes. Later illustration became increasingly complex and detailed, but was always characterized in the best Persian work by elegance of drawing and by decorative color and composition. In the sixteenth century the influence of Persian miniature painting, as well as of her other arts, became dominant in Turkey and India, giving rise to the highly finished painting of these regions.

BAHRUM GUR HUNTING
Miniature painting attributed to Mu'in Musawwir

JONAH AND THE WHALE
Mongol School, Late 14TH CENT.

ISLAMIC ART

LOVERS
Miniature signed by Riza-i-Abbasi. Persian, 16TH CENT.

THE EMPEROR AURANGZIB
Indian miniature, 1658–1707

ISLAMIC ART

OLD TESTAMENT KING FROM THE TREE OF JESSE
Panel from a stained-glass window.   Rhenish, c. 1300

THE CHRIST
Gold-enamel, Byzantine, 11TH CENT.

The Art of the Middle Ages

THE Roman Empire fell of its own weight. It was impossible, with the inadequate means of communication at its disposal, to keep together its far-flung peoples with their differences in race, creed and political inheritance. Civilization—that is Hellenistic-Roman civilization—crumbled; but it died slowly. The process took place so gradually that we see new forces and new ideas emerging and rising as quickly as the old institutions and beliefs were cast aside. The world of Alexander the Great had been completely transformed and the Hellenistic-Roman pattern of rationalism and logic, expressed in Greek architecture and Roman law, was infused with the irrational mysticism of Oriental faith and with the sense of common law and freedom of the individual so dear to the Barbarian tribes of Northern Europe. From this conflict rose the great nations of modern times and the spiritual empires of Christ and Mohammed which controlled the destinies of the later Middle Ages.

This drama of the Mediterranean basin was chiefly centered in the four great cities of the ancient world: Rome, Alexandria, Antioch and Byzantium (Constantinople). Athens, though still considered sentimentally the mainspring of Greek culture, had already sunk to the level of a provincial town. Rome, capital of the West, was the omnipotent forum of the Caesars and the seat of Latin Christianity. As yet

SAINT JOHN WRITING THE GOSPEL
Anglo-Frankish, c. 850. Pierpont Morgan Library

the cities of Europe were not developed, for they were no more than Visigothic and
Frankish villages built upon the abandoned campsites of Roman Gaul. Rome, however, had suffered an eclipse; she was dead as a cultural center of gravity, the pagan
gods were moribund. An artistic vacuum had been created in which the descriptive
and narrative attitude of the Graeco-Roman world toward art had run its course.
While tentative attempts had been made in the catacombs to pour the new wine of
Christianity into old pagan bottles, the artists of the early Church in Rome had failed
because the awakened interest in things of the spirit required a different symbolic
language. Obviously the saint must be depicted in other terms than the physical perfection of the athlete or nymph of classical antiquity. And too, such a symbolic expression could find nourishment only in a soil protected by a state religion.

When in A.D. 330 Constantine, who seven years earlier had formally adopted
Christianity, founded the capital of the Eastern Empire on the banks of the Bosphorus
and named it after himself, he insured the success of Byzantine rule for a thousand
years. Because of its favorable position on the highway between Europe and Asia, the

BUILDING OPERATIONS
French, c. 1250. Pierpont Morgan Library

city commanded the water passages between the Mediterranean and the Black Seas and became at once a logical center for a vast commerce which was protected by a large army and navy. The Byzantine Empire enjoyed a strong central administrative government and soon dominated Rome. The luxury and grandeur of the Byzantine court surpassed anything which the ancient world had seen since the days of the Pharaohs; and the Byzantine style, in the words of Eric Newton, gave the artist "for the first time an opportunity of *creating* a complete iconography of the visual side of religion" on church walls, and "not merely of *illustrating* it." Their greatest monument was the Church of Hagia Sophia (Santa Sophia or Divine Wisdom) erected by the Emperor Justinian in A.D. 537. Turned into a mosque after the fall of Constantinople in 1453, its magnificent mosaic decorations were plastered over and have been uncovered only within the past decades. The marble facing of the exterior, taken from abandoned Greek and Roman buildings, later was removed by the Venetians to embellish their Cathedral of Saint Mark.

While the Eastern Empire was rising to ever greater heights, the decay at Rome continued with frightening rapidity. The separation of the Empires of the East and West by Theodosius in A.D. 395 was, in a sense, the death sentence of Hellenistic-

Roman civilization. For nearly three centuries the Emperor was either at the battle front or in the newly established capital at Milan. He was seldom in Rome and then only for occasional triumphs. Burned by Nero and subjected to fire and pestilence, the city had sunk to a very low ebb. Morale went from bad to worse, and finally in 476 the Roman Empire of the West came to an end with the removal of the Emperor and the bestowal of his powers upon the Emperor of the East. Italy was divided into a series of Gothic kingdoms and Byzantine principalities, and the Latin Empire was not to be restored until the year 800 when Charlemagne was crowned Holy Roman Emperor.

While all of the forces of decay had been latent within the Roman administration, the rapidity of her collapse was accelerated by the Germanic invasions of the fifth century. The tall, blond Nordics from the Baltic, who inhabited rude huts and caves and lived a nomadic existence hunting and plundering, had long been a menace to the Roman legions which at the time of Hadrian had established their natural frontiers along the Rhine, the Danube and the Euphrates rivers. First the Goths under Alaric swept over Europe and sacked the city of Rome in 410. Then the Asiatic Huns, led by the terrible Attila, fell upon the Goths in Spain and southern Gaul. The Eastern Goths set up a kingdom in Italy under Theodoric; Celts and Franks filtered through the region of the lower Rhine to merge into a permanent race —the French. Angles, Saxons and Jutes made settlements in England while the Vandals, who were the last to sack Rome, in 455, roved as pirates from Spain and North Africa, constantly looting southern Italy and Sicily. In the north the Danes and other Vikings spread westward to the islands, while the Slavic tribes which had settled in Bohemia and the Danubian valley were in turn overcome by the Magyars.

The cultures of these nomadic tribes were very much alike. They lived close to nature and their art is largely decorative: magnificent woodcarvings for their rustic buildings and churches, grave objects of gold, silver and bronze, nervous flowing lines and interlacings with grotesque and beautiful use of animal forms. The Roman colonists accepted nearly as much from these barbaric craftsmen as they gave them in architecture and the arts.

The splendor and learning of the Byzantine rulers at Ravenna formed a vivid contrast to the rude art of the "Dark Ages." The Latin element derived from the last flush of Graeco-Roman art at Alexandria was based on the principle of representation. There, as may be seen in the frescoes from Boscoreale (pages 12 and 13), figures moved in real space; this conception was the survival of the Greek ideal of rational man, untrammeled by the joys or vicissitudes of everyday life. As opposed to this was the Byzantine concept which sought to revive the glories of Athenian art of the fourth and fifth centuries B.C., where the figure was removed and isolated from the background and rendered two-dimensionally. The hieratic majesty of the twelfth century mosaic image of the Mother of God in the Hagia Sophia (page 38) is the ultimate expression of the sculpture of the Parthenon carved well over a thousand years before. The third and last element, and one which was to blend the other two into a homogeneous Romanesque style was the barbaric naturalism of the North.

This fusion was not to take place until after the magical year 1000 when all good Christians had come to believe that the world might end. Their astonishment that it did not is expressed in the words of the chronicler Raoul Glaber, "It was as if the world, shaking off its tatters desired to re-clothe itself in the white robes of the Church . . . all religious buildings, cathedrals, country churches and village chapels were transformed by the faithful into something better." This something better is what today we call the Romanesque.

Romanesque art was essentially an art of stone carved in the round as opposed to the Byzantine architecture of brick covered with a surface veneer of marble or glass mosaic. Sculpture was confined to the decoration of portals and the capitals of columns on which were spread the lessons of the Old and New Testaments. When the pilgrimage centers gradually outgrew the Romanesque, the new Gothic style of building permitted the erection of larger churches, spanned by soaring groined vaults, whose lighter walls, supported by buttresses, could be interrupted by huge windows of stained glass which provided a new medium for decoration.

The principal source for the subject matter of medieval painting and sculpture was the illuminated manuscript. Already, from the time of Pope Gregory the Great in the sixth century, it had been the instrument of the Benedictine monks in keeping religion and culture alive among the Barbarians. Taking with them from their Mother House at Monte Cassino manuscripts of the Gospels, the Ordinary of the Mass and copies of the Rule of Saint Benedict, they established monasteries throughout Western Europe and Britain. They were thus responsible for the learning of feudal society, and their exquisitely illustrated books, meticulously copied again and again, became the source books for the medieval craftsmen who translated these images into stone, ivory and metal. They even enlarged them into sumptuous tapestries which were hung on the stone walls of abbeys and castles to keep out the cold.

By the thirteenth century the Gothic cathedral had become a visual encyclopedia of human knowledge. Carved and painted on its walls, and illustrated in its windows, were scenes from the Scriptures and the lives of the Saints, interspersed with animals and foliage and representations of the seasons, the arts and sciences, moral allegories and personifications of the Virtues and Vices. Chartres Cathedral, which contains no less than 10,000 such images, was the epitome in stone of Vincent de Beauvais's *The Mirror of the World*, written for St. Louis. As the age of feudalism declined, and the spirit of nationalism began to assert itself in Europe, naturalism, and the search for the sainted individual who bore the stamp of God upon his soul, became the preoccupation of the Gothic artist. Its effect upon domestic life and manners, and its reflection upon the household arts, will be seen in the unfolding of the Northern Renaissance.

AQUAMANILE, 12TH–13TH CENT.

CHALICE, 13TH CENT.

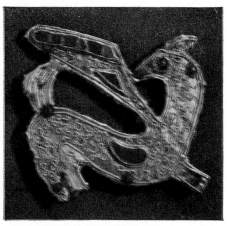

MEROVINGIAN FIBULA, 7TH CENT.

ITALIAN IVORY, 11TH CENT.

GERMAN IVORY, 10TH CENT.

MEDIEVAL MINOR ARTS (7TH–13TH CENT.)

ST. JAMES

GOTHIC VIRGIN

HEAD OF CHRIST

ROMANESQUE VIRGIN

VISITATION

MEDIEVAL SCULPTURE (12TH–14TH CENT.)

ALEXANDER THE GREAT (OR HECTOR?)

One of the Nine Heroes of medieval literature represented in a set of tapestries woven for Jean, Duke of Berry, in the workshop of Nicholas Batailles, Paris. End of the 14th century.

COUNTRY LIFE, French

ANNUNCIATION, French

UNICORN ENCLOSED, French

HECTOR LEGEND, French

COURTIERS WITH ROSES, Franco-Flemish

MEDIEVAL TAPESTRIES (14TH–15TH CENT.)

THE MOTHER OF GOD

After the original mosaic recently uncovered in the vault of the Eastern Apse of the Church of the Hagia Sophia (Divine Wisdom), Constantinople. Byzantine. 12th–14th century.

The Classical Renaissance

THE dawn of the Renaissance is usually placed at the beginning of the fifteenth century although its origins go back deep into the twelfth. But the beginnings of modern life came somewhat earlier in Italy than in the rest of Europe; for in the Western monarchies of France, England and Spain the feudal system, with its ties of fealty to the crown or to the overlord, retarded the rise of personal initiative. The Italian city-states had retained, at least in theory, the pattern of the classical republic in which the citizen felt free to overthrow a tyrant and replace him with another. Rich and powerful merchants controlled political life and waged merciless wars on one another with mercenary troops or *condottieri*. Aligning themselves now with the popular party of the Popes, the *Guelph*, now with the aristocratic followers of the German Emperor, the *Ghibellines*, they sold out to the highest bidder with all the cyncism expounded in Machiavelli's *The Prince*. A devastating Hundred Years' War between France and England, not to end until 1453, the year Constantinople fell to the Turks, had made Italy the broker between East and West, the center of profiteering and prosperity. Subduing her rivals Genoa and Pisa, Venice dominated the waterways to the Orient and developed as an independent republic, spreading her authority and her commerce over the Adriatic and Aegean Seas. Florence, led by such great banking families as the Medici, the Strozzi and the Pitti, rose to fame as the magnet which attracted to it all of the luxuries and the arts. The Visconti and Sforza ruled in Milan while Sigismondo Malatesta held power in Rimini, Federigo da Montefeltro in Urbino and in Ferrara the Este family. It was a new age of individualism and, in the Italian city-states, it was the glory and power of the individual that counted.

The significance of the Renaissance however, is not so much its rugged individualism or its return to classical forms as it is the revival of learning which accompanied it. In the classic phrase of Michelet, "the great achievements of the Renaissance were the discovery of the world and the discovery of man. . . . By discovery of the world is meant, on the one hand, the appropriation by civilized humanity of all corners of the habitable globe, and on the other, the conquest by Science of all that we know about the nature of the universe. In the discovery of man, again, it is possible to trace a twofold process. Man in his temporal relations, illustrated by Pagan antiquity, and man in his spiritual relations, illustrated by Biblical antiquity; these are the two regions . . . which the critical genius of the Renaissance opened for investigation."

It was inevitable that Rome should make the Renaissance her own. Not only did she have at her disposal the wealth of all Christendom, but she had as well the

MADONNA–CIMABUE (1240–1302)
Florence. The Uffizi (Artext Junior Print 193).

rich cultural soil in which the new humanism could grow. Emulating the merchant princes of Florence, the Church under Pope Nicholas V realized that architecture was the most effective means of expressing her greatness; and with Julius II, the Papacy became the chief vehicle for the dissemination of artistic ideas. Following in the footsteps of the Popes, the Cardinals rivaled one another in building magnificent churches, palaces and mausoleums.

Architects shared the desire to reawaken the classical past, borrowing from antiquity such elements as cornices, capitals, pilasters. But in the other arts the cult of the antique was at first confined to a small company of humanists intent on shaking off the fetters of medievalism. Artists as well as poets were later encouraged to create new and living forms based on classical foundations and soon they surpassed their models. The science of perspective, unknown to the ancient world, was a Renaissance achievement, making possible the correct representation of natural objects from a single viewpoint; it was an indispensable discovery for the development of modern painting. The evolution of the new style was gradual and its beginnings can be traced

FIFTY CENTURIES OF ART

THE BETRAYAL—GIOTTO

*These nearly life-size frescoes were painted in the Arena Chapel
at Padua in the North of Italy c. 1300.*

THE ENTRY INTO JERUSALEM—GIOTTO

in the Gothic buildings of the fourteenth century. Even in the fifteenth, Gothic elements survived, although by that time they were considered barbaric. First Tuscany took the leadership and Florence became the fountainhead of artistic life; Venice and Lombardy did not fully accept the new style until after 1450.

Italian artists experimented with new techniques. Murals were executed in fresco, a method of painting directly upon the wet plaster wall with dry, earthen water colors. It required both decision and rapidity for, drying instantly, it tolerated no retouching. Painters began to look at their subjects broadly and to generalize in form, color and composition. Flesh tints were done in dark ochres and reds with accentuated highlights to carry well at a distance and give a convincing sense of relief. The earliest masters were Cimabue, in Florence, and Duccio, in Siena, who painted in the last half of the thirteenth century and were both essentially Byzantine in character. The real founder of the Florentine School was, however, Giotto (1267?–1337) who introduced a new grandeur of conception and a spiritual force and pathos into his two great fresco cycles, the *Life of Christ* at Padua, and the *Legend of St. Francis* at Assisi. His ability to suggest form beneath drapery and to give his figures "living, tactile values," isolates him from his medieval contemporaries as the precursor of modern painting. Giotto dominated Florentine art for half a century and we have innumerable panel pictures by his followers, painted on panels of hard wood coated with gesso, or plaster; the technique employed was tempera, or distemper, in which dry colors, ground very fine, were moistened and held together with a binding medium or glue, usually white of egg.

Florence was the center of humanistic debate in science and theology. Perspective, the placing of figures in space, anatomy and the correctness of the drawing of the human figure were the artists' chief interest. It was the moment when the Medici were consolidating their power and Brunelleschi was developing his famous dome for the Cathedral. Ghiberti had won the competition for sculpturing the bronze doors of the Baptistry and Donatello was already leading the sculptors, both in marble and in bronze, to a realism not known since classical antiquity.

Siena remained more faithful to the Byzantine tradition; her art was more sensitive and spontaneous, closer to the heart than to the head. The followers of Duccio, Simone Martini and the Lorenzetti disregarded form and expressed themselves with emotional colors and a nervous, rhythmic calligraphic line. Although the Sienese school lost its vigor toward the middle of the century, these heartwarming qualities were passed on to the next generation of painters, Sassetta and Giovanni di Paolo, and in turn to their successors, Neroccio and Francesco di Giorgio. The Renaissance did not really touch Venice until the fall of Constantinople. Then with the advent of the brothers Bellini, Giovanni and Gentile, Andrea Mantegna and Vittore Carpaccio, her art was revolutionized.

ST. JEROME – BOTTICELLI
(1445–1510)

NATIVITY – FRA ANGELICO
(1387–1455)

MADONNA – SIGNORELLI
(1441–1523)

MADONNA – G. DI PAOLO

EPIPHANY – GIOTTO WORKSHOP

PAINTERS OF THE ITALIAN RENAISSANCE

MADONNA – G. BELLINI

MADONNA – C. CRIVELLI

ADORATION – MANTEGNA

HOLY FAMILY – MANTEGNA

ST. LAWRENCE – FRA LIPPO LIPPI

PAINTERS OF THE EARLY ITALIAN RENAISSANCE

THE VIRGIN AND CHILD–MANTEGNA (1431–1506)
Detail from the Adoration of the Shepherds
shown on the opposite page

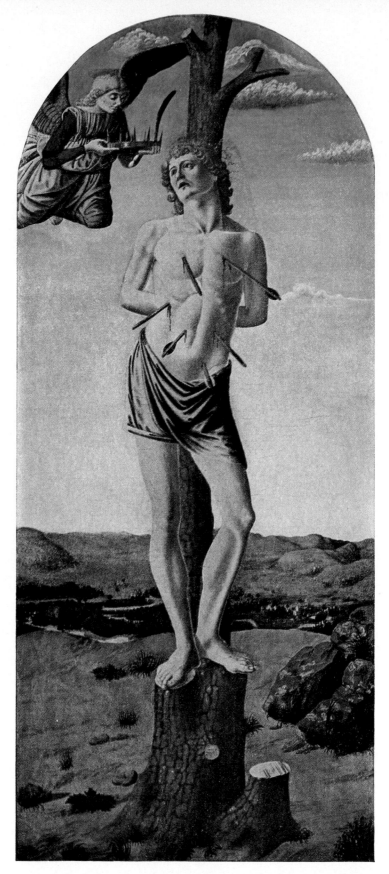

SAINT SEBASTIAN – ANDREA DEL CASTAGNO (1390?–1457)

*The anatomical interest in the representation of the Saint and the
depth of the landscape reflect the new scientific realism of Florence,
introduced by Masaccio, Masolino and Pollaiuolo after 1430.*

MAGNIFICAT–BOTTICELLI (1445–1510)
Florence. The Uffizi (Artext Junior Print 22)

THE JOURNEY OF THE MAGI–SASSETTA
Sienese. Early 15TH CENT.

MADONNA OF HUMILITY–FRA ANGELICO
Washington. The National Gallery of Art, Mellon Collection

Fra Angelico (1387–1455), a pious Dominican monk, one of the inspired men of the Renaissance, ascetic and mystic, accepted the budding naturalism of his day only in so far as it gave an outward expression to an inner spiritual life. He worked exclusively for his order, painting large murals in the Convent of San Marco in Florence where he spent his life, as well as smaller devotional images for the cells of the monks. His fame was such that Pope Nicholas V brought him to Rome to decorate his private chapel in the Vatican. Filled with compassion and tenderness, the bland tonality of his color is in keeping with the sentiments conveyed. It was said of him that when he fell asleep exhausted from his work the angels appeared and continued the painting upon which he was engaged.

Masolino da Panicale (1383–1447?) and his pupil Masaccio (1401–1429) present a vivid contrast to the piety of Fra Angelico. For it is with Masaccio that scientific curiosity supplants the dictates of the Church. He was frankly concerned with the new relation of an anatomically functional man to a physically real environment, seen moreover, in mathematically correct perspective. Masolino, while more rigid than the

FIFTY CENTURIES OF ART

ANNUNCIATION—MASOLINO DA PANICALE
Washington. The National Gallery of Art, Mellon Collection

younger Masaccio, was obsessed by the same curiosity. Already in the *Annunciation* the interpretation of motive and the rendering of individual form are more concretely expressed; landscape and buildings are no longer merely explanatory incidents to the composition; they are studied for themselves and are brought into proper balance with easily articulated figures that move in three dimensions. From this point on, the illusion of space, and the creation of plastic effects within that space, become the all-important problems for the Renaissance artist. Antonio del Pollaiuolo (1429?– 1498) and Andrea del Castagno (1390?–1457) were particularly occupied with them as was Luca Signorelli (1441–1523), whose almost Baroque portrayal of muscular distortion presaged the art of Michelangelo.

The artists of Italy were equally enthralled with the classical and pagan aspects of humanism. Lorenzo the Magnificent (1469–1492) continued the policies of his grandfather Cosimo and enjoyed the power and prestige of a prince, though he had neither the title nor the office. Under the protection of the Medici Florence had become a haven for refugee Greek scholars from Constantinople whom Cosimo employed

THE YOUTHFUL DAVID–CASTAGNO
Washington. National Gallery of Art, Widener Collection

to bring together the finest library of classic texts assembled since the library of the Ptolemys in Alexandria. Through them literary impetus given a century earlier by Dante, Petrarch and Boccaccio burst into full flower. The Medici palace on the Via Larga (now known as the Riccardi Palace) was the most celebrated and envied house in Europe and was called "the Hotel of the Princes of the whole world." It was in reality the first museum of modern times; sculptures, tapestries, paintings, bronzes, furniture and the most precious workmanship of goldsmith, enameler and jeweler were crowded into its rooms and galleries. These collections were available to the artists of the day, who came there to copy from the antique and to execute commissions in the new manner. The gods and goddesses of Olympus mingled there with Saints and Martyrs and the Fathers of the Church. Throughout Italy the lesser courts imitated the patronage and splendor of the Medici: Urbino, Mantua, Ferrara, Milan and even the Spanish Viceregal capital of Naples.

There is scarcely an artist, painter, architect, sculptor or goldsmith, of the second half of the fifteenth century who was not employed by the Medici. Fra Filippo

FIFTY CENTURIES OF ART

SPRING – BOTTICELLI
Florence. The Uffizi (Artext Junior Print 405)

*This picture, together with his Birth of Venus, is considered one of the
major documents of the pagan humanism of the Florentine Renaissance.*

Lippi, a more worldly monk than Angelico, his son Filippino Lippi, a pupil of Sandro
Botticelli, perhaps the most popular artist of the *Quattrocento*, the sculptor, Verrocchio,
a master of line and landscape in whose studio Leonardo da Vinci was apprenticed,
Domenico Ghirlandaio and Lorenzo di Credi were all members of this princely household. Their works have been preserved despite the mad efforts of the reformer Savonarola to burn such evidences of paganism and idolatry in the public square. The one
artist who best characterizes humanistic Florence is Sandro Botticelli; original, fantastic, passionate, he is the very quintessence of the Renaissance. In the words of
Louis Hourticq, "Without being a colorist, without even desiring to be one, he suc-
ceeds in emphasizing the continuous and contagious *tremolo* of his line by color."

In Umbria Piero della Francesca (1416–1492) was adding another element to
Renaissance art—the use of light and color as means of giving depth and solidity to
the forms within the picture. Medieval artists were little concerned with light, for
their flat figures cast no shadow. Piero, an accomplished mathematician, who dedicated his treatise on perspective to his patron, the Duke of Urbino, used light and
shadow to create mood. His frescoes depicting the *Legend of the Holy Cross* in the
Church of San Francesco at Arezzo, are the link between Masaccio's murals a genera-

THE RESURRECTION—PIERO DELLA FRANCESCA
Umbrian, 1465. Borgo San Sepolcro. Municipal Museum

tion earlier in Florence and Michelangelo's ceiling of the Sistine Chapel in Rome. Close by at Borgo San Sepolcro he painted the *Resurrection* (1465), often called the greatest masterpiece of Italian painting. The stark simplicity of the landscape, the monumental dignity of the centurions and the overwhelming drama of the risen Christ are bathed in a thin and supernatural light which models the forms, testifying to the artist's color sense and controlled imagination.

Piero's influence spread to Padua, and from there Mantegna carried these discoveries to Venice and northern Italy. Fra Carnevale, an architect and engineer attached to the Court of Urbino, painted closely in the style of Piero. One of the rare and exquisite panels attributed to him recalling the Arezzo frescoes is shown opposite.

The *Quattrocento* (1400 to 1500), a period of intellectual ferment like our own, was only the preparation for the Golden Age from the accession of Pope Julius II in 1503 to the Sack of Rome in 1527. The banishment of the Medici from Florence in 1494 for eighteen years had in no way diminished their enthusiasm for the arts; their activities were merely transferred to the Vatican where as cardinals and Popes they helped prepare the threshold for the supreme accomplishments of Raphael Sanzio of Urbino and Michelangelo Buonarroti. The other titan of this great triumvirate, Leonardo da Vinci, had already left Florence to make his fame and fortune in the service of

THE VISITATION—FRA CARNEVALE

*Detail from the Birth of the Virgin, Umbrian, 1456–1485. This painting shows
a Biblical scene placed in an elaborate setting of the early Renaissance.*

GIULIANO DE' MEDICI–BOTTICELLI
Berlin. Kaiser Friedrich Museum

Lodovico il Moro, the Duke of Milan, and Francis I, the King of France. At this moment Italy was torn asunder; the French and Spanish had entered into their death struggle for the domination of the peninsula. Columbus was bringing back reports of a new hemisphere across the seas; the Moors had been driven out of Spain and the Hapsburg dominions of Spain and the Low Countries were being incorporated into the Holy Roman Empire. Rome had become once more the capital of the world, the center of religion and finance, which chose to ignore the storm warnings of the Reformation coming out of Germany. Henry VII by his miserliness was laying the foundations for the wealth of Elizabethan England. Already shorn of Constantinople and her possessions in the Adriatic, Venice was on the eve of a further crushing naval defeat. Julius II, "the saviour of the Papacy and the curse of Italy," saw the culmination and fruition of two centuries of humanistic preparation. To him we owe splendid works of these artists and the very basilica itself of Saint Peter's, called by Symonds, "that materialized idea, which remains to symbolize the transition from the Church of the Middle Ages to the modern semi-secular supremacy of Papal Rome."

DUKE OF URBINO–PIERO DELLA FRANCESCA
Florence. The Uffizi

In 1503, the year of Julius' accession, Leonardo and Michelangelo were still working in Florence as were Perugino and his young pupil Raphael. Botticelli was fifty-nine years old, Perugino fifty-seven, Leonardo fifty-one, Michelangelo twenty-eight, and Raphael twenty. Among the others present in the city were Lorenzo di Credi, Fra Bartolommeo, Filippino Lippi and Andrea del Sarto, whom Vasari called "the perfect painter." Francia was at work in Bologna, Pinturicchio in Siena and Luini at Milan. Mantegna, Bellini, Carpaccio, Giorgione, Palma Vecchio, and Titian were setting the final jewels in the crown of Venice. Italy had become the envy of the civilized world, and, with the Interregnum in Florence bringing patronage to a stand-still, Rome had the pick of the most fabulous array of talent ever available in any one place at any one time.

Technical problems which had engrossed the artists of the *Quattrocento* had been mastered and a hundred years of humanism had liberated the painter from the bond-age of religious subject matter. While lip service was still given to the theologian and the scholar, the imagination had a chance to wander. Suddenly pictures became

THE SASSETTI PORTRAIT–D. GHIRLANDAIO

peopled with living individuals having personalities of their own. Since the primary concern of the Renaissance was the discovery of man, it was logical that the portrait should move out of the realm of the ideal to the concrete and the actual; thus we see figures moving through space who are no longer generalities or symbols but creatures of flesh and blood, whose individual character is revealed in their features. Portraiture, which had been dormant since ancient Rome, had once more come into its own.

Raphael Sanzio of Urbino, 1483–1520

Not the least of the miracles of this extraordinary age was the career of Raphael who, in the short thirty-seven years of his life, summarized and epitomized the entire course of Italian humanism. Born in Urbino, he worked in the atelier of Perugino in Perugia; later he learned anatomy, drawing and perspective from Leonardo in Florence where he produced his celebrated series of *Madonnas*, of which two, the *Alba*, now in Washington, and the *Colonna* at the Metropolitan, are shown here. In 1508

QVANTVM·HOMINI·FAS·EST·MIRA·LICET·ASSEQVAR·ARTE
NIL·AGO·MORTALIS·EMVIOR·ARTE·DEOS

PORTRAIT OF A LADY—NEROCCIO
Washington. National Gallery, Widener Collection

Pope Julius II brought him to Rome to decorate the *stanze*, or state apartments. After the succession of Leo X in 1513 he was entrusted with further commissions, appointed superintending architect of Saint Peter's, director of art at the Vatican and placed in charge of all antiquities in Rome. These positions he occupied until his death in 1520, and in addition found time to do the exquisite murals in the Farnesina and the Villa Madama.

The *Camera della Segnatura*, or Hall of the Seal, was the seat of these high tribunals of the papal court over which the Pope himself presided. Raphael conceived of its decoration as a visual library of humanism—"a public manifesto" of the powers and responsibilities of the Church in the four major areas of theology, philosophy (including science), the arts and the law. Three of these tremendous murals are shown in the following pages. The first, *La Dispulà* (The Disputation), presents an imaginary council of the Church in which theologians, surrounded by saints and prophets, discuss the Doctrine of the Transubstantiation of the Sacrament. The grandeur of the composition, in which all points converge on the Eucharist and the Trinity above it, is a conception which reflects the genius of the painter and the maturity of the time in

THE "COLONNA MADONNA"–RAPHAEL

*This great altarpiece painted in 1505 for a convent in Perugia was long known
in the Colonna Palace in Rome and in the collection of the Kings of Naples.
It was presented to the Metropolitan Museum by J. Pierpont Morgan.*

THE CRUCIFIXION – PERUGINO
Washington. The National Gallery of Art, Mellon Collection

which he lived. He is equally at home in the *The School of Athens* (*Philosophy*), where, in a setting recalling Bramante's design for the new Saint Peter's which was currently being erected, there is an assembly of the great philosophers and natural historians of the ancient world led by Plato and Aristotle. In *Parnassus*, the mural devoted to the arts, Apollo and the Muses sit in an idyllic landscape surrounded by the poets of antiquity and the humanists of Italy. The painting of *The Law* (not illustrated here) presents personifications of the three virtues of justice: *Prudence*, *Temperance* and *Fortitude*. Certainly up to this time Europe had seen no such encyclopedic statement or summary of the disparate elements which, fused together, marked the transition from the Middle Ages to modern times.

Raphael was both the culmination and the conclusion of a long tradition, and what we tire of today is not his art but the adulation which the nineteenth century showered upon it. In the four hundred years which separate us no new fundamental problem in painting was to arise until the 1860's, when the *Impressionists* in Paris began to investigate the effects of sunlight on the artist's palette. To be sure, a glorious procession of schools and geniuses were to leave their impact on the post-Renaissance centuries; but throughout Europe the best artists of the *Baroque* and *Rococo* as highly gifted individuals were either improving or commenting upon the Italian Renaissance. It is the strength, and at the same time the weakness, of Raphael that modern art, as he understood it, began and ended with him.

PARNASSUS

THE CLASSIC POETS, From the Parnassus

RAPHAEL'S FRESCOES IN THE "STANZE" OF THE VATICAN

THE SCHOOL OF ATHENS

THE DISPUTATION

RAPHAEL'S FRESCOES IN THE "STANZE" OF THE VATICAN

MADONNA–VERROCCHIO

LADY–LORENZO DI CREDI

THE BAPTIST–PIERO DI COSIMO

CHESS PLAYERS–FRANCESCO DI GIORGIO

HOLY FAMILY–A. DEL SARTO

ITALIAN PAINTERS OF THE RENAISSANCE

NEGRESS, 16TH CENT.

CHARLES V, 6TH CENT.

SAVONAROLA, Medal, 15TH CENT.

MADONNA – L. DELLA ROBBIA

CUP – BENVENUTO CELLINI (?)

RENAISSANCE DECORATIVE ARTS

THE "ALBA" MADONNA–RAPHAEL

*Washington. The National Gallery of Art, Mellon Collection.
Formerly in the collections of the Dukes of Berwick and Alba,
and later in the Hermitage at Saint Petersburg, it was sold by
the Soviet Government.*

APOLLO–GIULIO ROMANO (?)

*Fresco decoration by one of Raphael's assistants from a villa
on the Palatine, Rome. The style is similar to the decorations of
the Loggie of the Vatican, executed under Raphael's direction.*

THE HOLY FAMILY—MICHELANGELO
Florence. The Uffizi

Michelangelo, 1475–1564

The essential difference between the temperaments of these two almost super-human geniuses, Raphael and Michelangelo, is possibly best summed up in a comparison of the *tondi* that face each other on these pages. Raphael has expressed in the *Alba Madonna* all that was smug and complacent in the full-blown Renaissance; the opulence of the forms and the glowing placidity of the color, a sweetness and contentment which, in anything less noble, would border on the cloying and the sentimental. It is the quintessence of descriptive painting, a gift which ranks him foremost among the illustrators of the world. Michelangelo, within the same circular limitations of the *tondo*, has invested the *Holy Family* with a tortured, sculptural anxiety which lifts it from the realm of illustration to the level of a profound personal experience. It is, in fact, one of the very few panel pictures by his hand for, with the exception of the Sistine Chapel murals which he executed under duress, throughout his life he preferred to think of himself as a sculptor rather than as a painter or architect. His preeminence in all three fields was not so much a matter of choice as it was the need to release his volcanic and convulsive emotions in whatever channel the moment dictated.

Another quality that set Michelangelo apart from his contemporaries was the depth of his Christianity. Whereas his fellow pupils who were studying with Bertoldo, in the art school which Lorenzo the Magnificent had established in his gardens of "good and antique sculpture," had succumbed to the fashionable paganism of Flor-

DAVID–MICHELANGELO
Florence. Academy

ence, Michelangelo did not let his preoccupation with the classical beauty of the human body lead him away from the religious and spiritual content of the story which, as an artist, employed by God's Vicar, he was called upon to tell. Thus he added to classical form those lingering medieval concerns with sin and the life to come which were to become the basic issues of the impending Reformation. It was his particular contribution to the evolution of art to be able to convey the torture of the soul through the muscular distortion of the body. The phrase "tragic and pathetic athletes" has been aptly used to denote the creations of this solitary misanthrope who was so uncompromising in his personal relations that he shared with Pope Julius II the reputation for *terribilità*.

Fleeing from Florence in 1494 with his exiled Medici patrons, Michelangelo resided briefly in Rome, where he carved the poignant *pietà* in Saint Peter's. In 1501 he returned to his native city to hew out of an ungainly block of marble, abandoned forty years earlier by Agostino di Duccio, the colossal *David*. The aged Pope, already sensing a premonition of death, brought him back to Rome at the beginning of his reign to start work upon his tomb—a task which, because of constant changes and

THE DYING CAPTIVE – MICHELANGELO
Paris. The Louvre

interruptions, occupied him during most of his life. The Pope, overcoming the sculptor's objections, also ordered him to paint in fresco the ceiling of the Sistine Chapel. This he accomplished between 1508 and 1512, the very years in which Raphael was decorating the *stanze*. His first love, however, was always sculpture. In the elements from the tomb of Julius II, the *Moses*, supposed to be a scathing impressionistic portrait of the Pontiff, and the *Dying Captive* in the Louvre, it is clear that Michelangelo used the classical figure merely as a point of departure; in the one, there emerges from the marble the wrath and majesty of the Old Testament, in the other, the abysmal despair and frustration of mortal man. A more mature sculptor appears in the tombs of Giuliano, Duke of Nemours and his cousin, Lorenzo, Duke of Urbino, which Michelangelo carved for the Medici Chapel in San Lorenzo in the years 1520–1534 when he was once more in Florence.

These tombs, which are quite similar, are composed of sarcophagi, upon which recline symbolic figures of *Day* and *Night*, *Dawn* and *Evening*, surmounted by idealized portraits of the deceased in niches; they are among the most moving and contemplative sculptures produced in any age. The severe architectural setting, designed

MOSES–MICHELANGELO
Tomb of Pope Julius II, San Pietro in Vincoli

by Michelangelo himself, enhances the timeless and cosmic reality of life and death. Here we see that utter disregard for sculptural convention which caused him to leave unfinished, as in the figure of *Day*, anything that was irrelevant. Thought and emotion grow out of the very stone itself; and how skillfully he has used the theme of one tomb as a foil for the other, Giuliano the man of action and Lorenzo the philosopher. The reclining men and women express the antithesis between human energy and crushing weariness, desire and renunciation. At no time in the history of art has the dignity of resignation been more wonderfully portrayed.

It is essential to understand Michelangelo the sculptor before examining his murals, for even in this medium it is plasticity which is paramount; he continues, as a French critic has put it, "to hurl creatures into space which are suspended neither in air nor in the atmosphere, but are simply sculptures in the round."

Michelangelo spent his life wrestling with the mysteries of God's universe. When Paul III appointed him chief architect of Saint Peter's he refused payment, declaring that he would "labor for the love of God and out of reverence for the Apostle."

FIFTY CENTURIES OF ART

TOMB OF GIULIANO–MICHELANGELO
Florence. The Medici Chapel, San Lorenzo

The Sistine Chapel in the Vatican is the chapel of the Pope from which the great pronouncements of the Church are made before consistories of the College of Cardinals, and where the latter are locked in conclave to elect a new Pontiff. Julius II was fully conscious that in his program of embellishment to give the Church the grandeur and dignity that the troubled times demanded he could find no more capable artist than Michelangelo to carry out the task of decorating this chapel, nor one better able to speak for the Church. For this reason he was willing to defer the completion of his own tomb and obliged the artist to proceed with the painting. The chapel is a narrow, long rectangular room (132 feet×44 feet) surmounted by a vaulted ceiling some seventy feet above the floor. The ceiling comprises a surface of approximately ten thousand square feet. Michelangelo, dissatisfied with the performance of his assistants, whom he immediately dismissed and whose work he destroyed, painted the area entirely with his own hand. Here he spread before an astonished world the age-old theme of the Christian faith—the creation, sin and redemption of mankind, the majesty of God and the beauty of man created in his image.

FIFTY CENTURIES OF ART

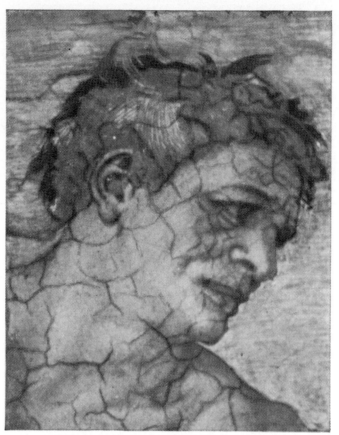

THE HEAD OF ADAM—MICHELANGELO
Detail from the Temptation and Expulsion, Sistine Ceiling

Nine major panels illustrate the first nine chapters of *Genesis*, beginning with *God Separating Light from Darkness* over the high altar and ending with *The Drunkenness of Noah*, opposite. Smaller compositions corresponding with the spandrels between the windows are devoted to representations of the ancestors of Jesus, the Prophets of the Old Testament and the Sibyls of classic Latin literature who were thought to have foretold the coming of Christ. Although no original painting or sculpture by Michelangelo can be seen in American collections, a precious red chalk drawing, a study for the *Libyan Sibyl*, was acquired some years ago by the Metropolitan Museum. Since it was a preliminary sketch, the artist began his thinking with an undraped male model. This is characteristic of his approach to a given problem and confirms his primary obsession with classic sculpture. Color, though always beautiful and harmonious, was a secondary consideration, a means of projecting the human figure from the wall, a tonal background for the painted, animated, life-size nudes of which, not counting cherubs and *putti*, there are over three hundred in the ceiling.

CHRIST AND THE MADONNA—MICHELANGELO
Detail from The Last Judgment, Sistine Chapel

Years later, between 1536 and 1541, when he was called once more to Rome by Pope Paul III, Michelangelo painted the great mural of the *Last Judgment* on the end wall over the high altar. Executed in the same massive tortured style, a miracle of foreshortening and *contrapposto*, the scene (of which only a detail is shown here) depicts the Christ appearing in Judgment accompanied by the Host of Heaven. In the lunettes above there are angels with instruments of the Passion, while below, in the middle register, more angels with trumpets are heralding the end of the earth. The separation of the damned and of God's elect is taking place while immediately below them the dead are rising from their tombs and Charon is seen ferrying the souls of the damned across the River Styx to Minos, Prince of Hell, who awaits them on the other side.

The *Last Judgment* thus completes the cycle of Christian dogma that Michelangelo conceived as the message of the Sistine Chapel decorations. Beginning with the *Creation* and the *Fall* of man, it continues with the Mosaic and Messianic dispensations and closes with the Trump of Doom.

THE LIBYAN SIBYL–MICHELANGELO
Detail of the Sistine Chapel Ceiling

THE LIBYAN SIBYL–MICHELANGELO
Drawing. Metropolitan Museum of Art

THE CUMAEAN SIBYL—MICHELANGELO
Another prophecy of the coming of Christ, Sistine Ceiling

It is prophetic that on the eve of the Council of Trent an artist was able to say in four years what the assembled Bishops of the Church were unable to say in twenty. Michelangelo was the herald of the reform within the Church. It was inevitable that those who came after him should, under the stimulus of the Jesuits, merely repeat *ad infinitum* these simply stated truths in the imitative mannered style of the Baroque.

THE CREATION OF ADAM

THE TEMPTATION AND EXPULSION FROM EDEN

SCENES FROM MICHELANGELO'S FRESCOES, SISTINE CHAPEL

THE CREATION OF THE SUN AND MOON

THE DELUGE (Left Side)

SCENES FROM MICHELANGELO'S FRESCOES, SISTINE CHAPEL

THE BAPTISM OF CHRIST—VERROCCHIO
Florence. Uffizi. Kneeling angel at left by the young Leonardo

The Apotheosis of Man: Leonardo da Vinci

If it fell to the lot of Raphael to illustrate and summarize the humanism and learning of Italy, and to Michelangelo to be the spokesman for the inner emotional and religious conflict of the age, it was Leonardo da Vinci (1452–1519) who was to express in his life and in his works the ultimate achievement of the Renaissance— the discovery of the world and the discovery of man. It has frequently been said of him that he was the first modern man, and, indeed, he was, in the sense that his judgments were rational and unbiased, based upon observation and personal experience rather than upon tradition. He was as George Sarton has said "a great artist trying to do his very best as a painter, a perfectionist; a man of science, anxious to find the truth, to understand God and nature, himself, and other men. . . . Think of him as a builder of bridges—one between science and art and another between the inchoate medieval thought and modern rationalism."

As an artist he was not content to be a painter; he mastered all the arts, including poetry and music. Architect, engineer, inventor of mechanical engines of war, expert on hydraulics, designer of the first airplane, his interests took him into the study of anatomy and physiology and into the mysteries of embryology and the dis-

76   **FIFTY CENTURIES OF ART**

THE ANNUNCIATION–LEONARDO DA VINCI
Florence. The Uffizi

section of the human brain. He was, in short, the universal man—the ideal creature of the Florentine Renaissance for whom the two centuries that separated him from Dante were but a period of anticipation and preparation.

He was the contemporary of Botticelli, born seven years his junior although in spirit they were centuries apart; the one brought the Middle Ages to a close, the other ushered in the modern world. Leonardo died in the arms of the King of France at Amboise in 1519, at the very moment when Raphael and Michelangelo were completing their decorations at the Vatican. Except for a brief encounter with him in Florence in their youth, they had but little contact with him.

THE LAST SUPPER–LEONARDO DA VINCI
Milan. Santa Maria delle Grazie

77

VIRGIN AND ST. ANNE–LEONARDO DA VINCI
Paris. The Louvre

Leonardo was apprenticed to Verrocchio at the age of thirteen, where he learned the sculptor's craft in addition to those of bronzecaster, goldsmith, draughtsman and painter. He remained with him for ten years not wishing to leave Florence to enter the service of the Duke of Milan until he was past thirty. Impractical in money matters, a dreamer and inventor, he perfected his art and jotted down in the precious notebooks which have come down to us the results of his investigations and experiments. The pictures that have been preserved are few, only eighteen in all, and if it were not for the notebooks and splendid series of drawings, the greater part of which are in the Royal Library at Windsor Castle, we would know little of his art. No generally accepted painting by his hand is in America; there are, however, a few splendid drawings in the Metropolitan Museum and in private possession. Since he passes lightly over his talents as an artist in his famous letter applying for a position with the implacable Sforza, wherein he emphasizes his abilities as a military engineer, painting must have been for him a more or less private means of expression. His greatest contributions to it are twofold: first, he revealed the manner in which chiaroscuro,

THE MONA LISA–LEONARDO DA VINCI
Paris. The Louvre

the technique of playing alternately with deep transparent shadows, could bathe the picture with atmosphere and light to express a mood. With him the brittle dryness of primitive delineation gave way to the subtleties and mystery of modern drawing. The other unique quality which he transmitted to all his work came from his conviction that painting was *"cosa mentale,"* a mental thing. It could not stop at being decorative but must be the vehicle for the translation into plastic terms of human sentiment and passion.

ADORATION OF THE SHEPHERDS–GIORGIONE

This celebrated painting has been frequently attributed to Titian's early period.
Washington. The National Gallery of Art, Kress Collection.

The Venetian Renaissance

THE Renaissance entered Venice by way of Padua which had become the intellectual center of Northern Italy because of the establishment there in the thirteenth century of its famous university. Andrea Squarcione, a painter and passionate antiquarian, one of the earliest collectors of classical statuary in Europe, had created in Padua, together with Jacopo Bellini, the father of Giovanni and Gentile, a school of artists which attracted to it Donatello and other masters from Tuscany and Umbria who were imbued with the New Learning. Under their influence the Vivarini, the Crivelli, and Antonello da Messina (who was reported to have learned the secret of oil painting from the Fleming, Petrus Christus) adapted the technical discoveries of Florence and the Low Countries to the rich and sensuous color of Byzantium. Giovanni Bellini's circle, Marco Basaiti, Cima da Conegliano and Vittore Carpaccio continued and spread the influence of the school. But it was Giovanni's brother, Gentile Bellini, a traveller to Constantinople with firsthand knowledge of the East, and his

THE FEAST OF THE GODS–GIOVANNI BELLINI
Washington. The National Galley of Art, Widener Collection

brother-in-law Andrea Mantegna, who formulated the direction Venetian art was to
take (see pages 42 and 43). Giovanni Bellini, born in 1430, lived to the age of eighty-
six and therefore bridged the gulf between the primitives of the fifteenth century and
the mature style of Giorgione, Titian, Tintoretto, and Veronese.

Giorgione's painting is, perhaps, more poetic, more somber and reflective than
that of Titian. It also shows a little less of the opulent and carnal paganism of the
latter's mythological nudes; but except for this spiritual reticence their artistic iden-
tities are difficult to keep apart.

Tiziano Vecelli (1477–1576), called *il Tiziano* or "the Titian," was born in the
village of Cadore in the Veneto where he developed an attachment to the Alpine
landscape that appears nostalgically in so many of his pictures. His incredibly long
career, in which he was active right up to his ninety-ninth year, is divided into three
quite clearly defined stages. The early years before 1518 cover his association with
Bellini and Giorgione in Padua and Venice. To this era belong his tentative efforts
as a fresco painter, as well as the murals in oil in the Doge's Palace and the early
Madonnas and the *Sacred and Profane Love* in the Borghese Gallery in Rome. The
second period, from 1518 to 1532, saw him largely in the service of the courts of
Mantua, Ferrara and Urbino, where he painted among a host of others the heavenly
bacchanalian pictures in Madrid and the London *Ariadne*. The last forty-four years of
Titian's life, from 1532 to 1576, were spent as a member of the household of his inti-

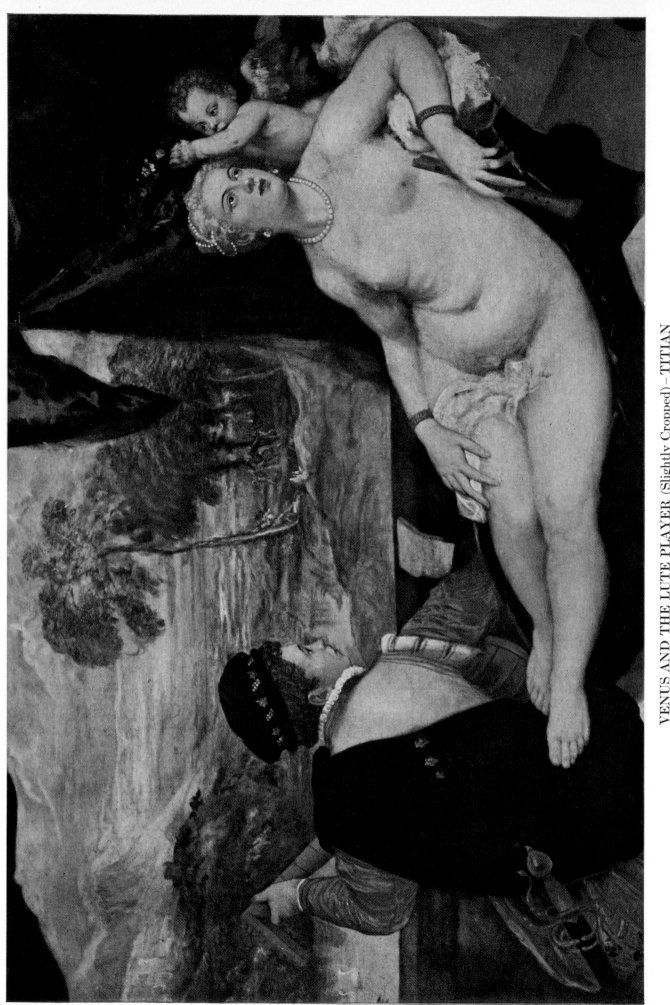

VENUS AND THE LUTE PLAYER (Slightly Cropped) – TITIAN

Besides this painting in The Metropolitan Museum of Art there are other versions by Titian in Vienna and Madrid

WORSHIP OF VENUS
Madrid. The Prado

VENUS AND ADONIS

THE MADONNA AND CHILD

THE ART OF TITIAN

DANAË AND THE SHOWER OF GOLD – TITIAN
Vienna. Kunsthistorisches Museum

mate friend the Hapsburg Emperor Charles V, who ennobled him, and of the latter's son the future King Philip II of Spain. An incomparable series of portraits, allegorical and religious pictures, painted either at Augsburg or in Venice, has been preserved chiefly in the Vienna Gallery and in Madrid, where the Prado alone has fifty-six canvases by his hand. The Metropolitan's reclining *Venus and the Lute Player* (reproduced on p. 82), of which there are other versions in Florence and Madrid, reveals Titian in the full maturity of his later years—the "subdued tonality, the easy broad composition, the deliberate leaving of unfinished portions, and the advanced aerial treatment of the landscape," giving a natural ease and sense of well being hitherto unfamiliar in European art.

While the political ambitions of the Doges were utterly crushed at the great naval battles of Lepanto and Agnadello, Venice, "the jewel of the Adriatic," continued to be one of the richest, if not the richest city in Europe until the eighteenth century. It was not difficult amidst so much luxury, where the oligarchy was obliged to impose sumptuary laws to keep ordinary citizens from dressing too extravagantly, to carry forward throughout the sixteenth century the taste for deep colors and satin textures with which Titian so magnificently enveloped his creations. His immediate followers seized upon his heritage and conspired to make the Venetians the foremost colorists of the world.

It was upon the shoulders of Paolo Caliari, called *il Veronese* (1528–1588), and Jacopo Robusti, called *il Tintoretto* (1518–1594), that the mantle of Elijah was to

FIFTY CENTURIES OF ART

SUSANNA AND THE ELDERS—TINTORETTO
Vienna. Kunsthistorisches Museum

fall. Veronese, the younger of the two, was less violent, bringing from his native city of Verona something of the blandness which Leonardo at Milan had bequeathed to the schools of Northern Italy. He was one of the greatest formal decorators that ever lived, as may be seen from a study of the two vast canvases the *Marriage of Cana* in the Louvre and the *Feast at the House of Levi* in the Academy in Venice. There we see assemblages of serene and proud patricians, stage managed with the utmost skill, parading in architecture borrowed from Palladio and Sansovino. But though he gave to oil painting something of the illustrative amplitude which Raphael gave to fresco, his work sometimes lacks the invention and brilliant color effects so beautifully displayed in the Metropolitan's *Mars and Venus United by Love*.

Tintoretto, the only one of the trinity born in the lagoons, burned with a fever of activity and restlessness. Taking up the palette of Titian's advanced years when the latter had abandoned his familiar russet golden tones in favor of silvery grays and blues as a foil for his more brilliant colors, Tintoretto applied his nervous energy to the study of the propulsion of the human figure through space. This is the preoccupation of the murals of Santa Maria dell' Orto and the Scuola di San Rocco.

Meanwhile in the rest of the peninsula the Renaissance was over and the arts were at a standstill. Italy had ceased to be a world power and the disintegration of the several states had already paved the way for the two centuries of disunion which was not to end until the time of Garibaldi. The Papacy alone held the disparate elements together and Rome entered upon her second Augustan Age, in which she became more of an academy than a creative center. The Reformation had broken on the Catholic world and the Jesuits were calling upon the Baroque artists to put their badly shaken institution in a more popular light. Florence was abandoned to the Mannerists, the uninspired imitators of Raphael and Michelangelo; Venice was a law unto herself; Correggio was forming a school at Parma which would influence French art in the next century. In Bergamo the Cariani were active and in Brescia Savoldo, Romanino and Moretto were producing portraits of a very high order.

The last twilight of the Renaissance glowed, however, in Rome and in the Bolognese Academy, founded as a corrective to the decadence of the Mannerists, whose eclectic art was "proof of their science rather than of their soul." The Carracci, Lodovico and his cousins Agostino and Annibale, were noted for an austere and formal sincerity in contrast with a freer romanticism in Albano, Guercino and Domenichino.

The rather dismal classicism of the Carracists was at last challenged by an uneducated plasterer, Caravaggio (1569–1609) who sought a return not to the smiling and serene naturalism of the late Renaissance but rather to the brutal and ugly squalor of the streets. Caravaggio was the first Italian to forsake idealism, and in the effects of lighting which he obtained by opening a trap door in the roof of his darkened studio, he subsequently earned the reputation of being the Manet of his day.

As the embers of the Renaissance were dying out with only a fitful burst of flame here and there—Strozzi in Genoa, Bronzino and Gentileschi in Florence, Maratta and Pannini in Rome—Venice at least preserved a freshness and vigor well into the eighteenth century. Tiepolo animated and revivified the legacy of Veronese, while a group of painters of fashion like Longhi, and specialists in the unique architectural water landscapes of Venice, such as Canaletto, his nephew Bellotto, Guardi and Marieschi, rang down the curtain on the five-hundred-year pageant of Italian art.

FEAST AT THE HOUSE OF LEVI—VERONESE
Venice. Academy (Artext Junior Print 130) (Detail)

MARS AND VENUS UNITED BY LOVE – VERONESE
Detail from the picture in The Metropolitan Museum of Art

THE FINDING OF MOSES—TINTORETTO

MEDITATION—CARPACCIO

DOGE AND THE REDEEMER—TINTORETTO

CHRIST IN THE WILDERNESS—M. DA BRESCIA

PAINTERS OF THE VENETIAN RENAISSANCE

COLUMBUS—S. DEL PIOMBO

YOUNG MAN—BRONZINO

PRIORESS—MORONI

YOUNG MAN—GIORGIONE (?)

GIRL WITH CHERRIES—PREDIS

PORTRAITS OF THE HIGH RENAISSANCE

THE LUTE PLAYER—STROZZI (1581–1644)

THE ANNUNCIATION—CORREGGIO (1494–1534)
Chalk drawing on pink paper

"MUSICA" (or THE MUSICIANS) – CARAVAGGIO (1569–1609)

"Italian Painting suddenly declined for lack of taste. The followers of Raphael and Michelangelo possessed astonishing power and knowledge, but, save their own cleverness, no longer had anything to express. Thus painting became merely an art of self-exploitation and display, a matter of difficult foreshortenings, complicated groupings, and novel constructions in light and shade."—Mather

AURORA – GUIDO RENI (1575–1642)
Rome. Rospigliosi Palace (Artext Junior Print 98)

SACRIFICE OF ABRAHAM—TIEPOLO

SCHLOSSHOF PALACE—BELLOTTO
Vienna. Kunsthistorisches Museum

THE MEETING—LONGHI

VENETIAN PAINTERS OF THE EIGHTEENTH CENTURY

SANTA MARIA DELLA SALUTE – CANALETTO

In Venice in the eighteenth century there arose a new type of water city-scape which became increasingly popular and was particularly adapted to the carnival life of the Republic. Both Canaletto and his contemporary Guardi were greatly influenced by Pannini's imaginative views of Rome.

THE CRUCIFIXION—HUBERT VAN EYCK

*Detail from the famous diptych of the Crucifixion and the Last
Judgment, formerly in the Imperial Gallery of the Hermitage
in Saint Petersburg. Acquired by The Metropolitan Museum
of Art after it was sold by agents of the Soviet Government.*

BETROTHAL OF ST. CATHERINE – MEMLING

The Northern Renaissance

THE Hundred Years War between France and England was scarcely a war of nations as we understand the term today; for the two nations hardly existed at all. They were gigantic fiefs or pawns in a never-ending struggle that had run its course since the invasion of Britain by William the Conqueror in 1066. The color and romance, the passions and the fury are fully recounted in Froissart and in Shakespeare's tragedies of the English kings. It was a saga of regicide and civil war in which the blood shed for the white rose of York and the red rose of Lancaster was matched only by the carnage of the opposing branches of the House of Valois. The gift by King John II, *le Bon*, in the middle of the fourteenth century, of the powerful and violently rival duchies of Burgundy, Berry and Anjou to his three sons as appanages, was the grand and empty gesture which resulted in the near suicide of the French monarchy —a crisis from which it did not recover until Joan of Arc finally drove the English from the continent and the "Spider King" Louis XI crushed the power of Burgundy and reestablished the French nation.

Into this pattern of feudal strife and jealousy the sophistication of Italian life had barely penetrated. It was an age of retarded medievalism which had begun with Chaucer, was immortalized in the poems of François Villon and was to end with Rabelais. Moreover the Valois princes, in every branch of that house, were, after the Medici and the Hapsburgs, the most zealous protectors of the arts and the most sensitive collectors and connoisseurs that Europe had produced. They set the stage for

CHRIST APPEARING TO HIS MOTHER
ROGIER VAN DER WEYDEN

THE STIGMATA–JAN VAN EYCK
Philadelphia Museum of Art. Johnson Collection

ANNUNCIATION–JAN VAN EYCK

ARNOLFINI MARRIAGE PORTRAIT–JAN VAN EYCK
London. The National Gallery

that glorious final outburst of Gothic architecture known on the continent as flamboyant and in England as the perpendicular.

The economic freedom so characteristic of the maritime capitalists of the Adriatic seaports and the early industralists of Tuscany was never tolerated by the French or Flemish nobleman. He exercised a dictatorial paternalism over the officers and petty officials of his court to which were attached not only the clergy and courtiers and men-at-arms, but also laborers and craftsmen, artisans and tradesmen. To maintain his traditional authority the noble had to be the embodiment of chivalry and the fountainhead of learning and the arts.

Heroic efforts of the nobility to keep merchants and peasants in their places were not enough to stem the tide of the rising middle class. In fact, the struggle for personal liberty and the coming to power of the guilds and corporations to assume the role they had earlier won in Germany and Italy became in France and Flanders the chief political issue of the fifteenth century.

As a result of social change domestic architecture underwent the same alterations which had taken place in the design of ecclesiastical buildings. Little by little, the

FIFTY CENTURIES OF ART

VIRGIN AND CHILD–GERARD DAVID
Philadelphia Museum of Art. Johnson Collection

fortified castle in which the feudal prince had entrenched himself gave way to the walled town or city. Sumptuous *hôtels particuliers*, or town houses, erected by the upstart burghers outshone the magnificence of the houses of the hereditary nobles who, when the monarchy was weak, were a constant threat to the crown. The *châteaux forts* were systematically destroyed by the King and in their places there arose along the Valley of the Loire the exquisite *châteaux de plaisance* which recalled the palaces and villas of Italy.

Franco-Flemish art, then, is the expression of a new type of urbanism which was the prelude to the industrialization of Europe during the next five hundred years. But, unlike Italy, the model that inspired it was not the republican City of Rome but rather Saint Augustine's City of God. Piety and mysticism are curiously blended with the ruthlessness of commerce and free enterprise; man's conscience and his anxiety for the future of his soul in after life shine through every work of art in which "the extremes of mysticism and gross materialism meet." A portrait by Rogier van der Weyden differs from one by Piero della Francesca in its approach to the prob-

A YOUNG WOMAN–VAN DER WEYDEN
Berlin. Kaiser Friedrich Museum

lem of reality. Piero's realism is universal and generic. The portrait of Federigo da Montefeltro (see p. 55) is more than the likeness of the *condottiere* of Urbino; it is the collective classical portrait of the prince, and bears the same relation in the visual arts that Machiavelli's *Prince* bears to individuals in history. Not so with the Flemish painter, whose portraits record an intimate knowledge of the sitter. An equally telling contrast may be recognized in the differences between the religious pictures of the North and South; to the Italian painter an altarpiece was an opportunity to convey through the means of a formal composition some philosophical or abstract idea, a teaching of the Church. To the Fleming it was a vehicle for sharing with the spectator an inner mystical experience.

At first, artistic activity was centered about the towns of Bruges and Ghent, whose wealth was derived primarily from the weaving of wool imported from the British Isles. Later, as the merchants prospered and the carrying trade with Portugal and the Orient made Antwerp the center of the silk and spice trade, artistic activity shifted there. The fame of the artists of the Low Countries spread all over Europe.

FIFTY CENTURIES OF ART

Imagiers, sculptors in wood and alabaster, traveled to Spain and Portugal; they created the Nottingham School in England and they were in constant demand in Eastern France and the Dauphiné. Flemish artists became, in fact, as much an article of export as the figures which they carved and gilded.

Tradition insists that the secret of oil painting was discovered in Flanders by the brothers van Eyck, who were the founders of the Flemish School. Actually the method had been known since the twelfth century, but the Flemings were probably the first to perfect drying media to give them a new splendor and intensity of color. And, as may be seen in the tiny *Saint Francis*, the van Eycks were the first to transform the art of the parchment illuminator to the nobler stature of the panel picture. Little is known of Hubert van Eyck, to whom are attributed the panels of the Last Judgment and The Crucifixion, beyond the controversial inscription on the frame of the great altarpiece, *The Adoration of the Lamb*, in the Cathedral of Saint Bavon at Ghent. This inscription states that it was begun by Hubert and completed by his brother, in 1432. Jan van Eyck (1390?–1441) is less elusive; he was court painter and *valet de chambre* to Philip the Good, Duke of Burgundy, who sent him on diplomatic missions to Portugal, Spain and The Hague. His primary interest was in realism, "a realism in which the soul is inseparable from the body, the spiritual from the visible, the inner life from the life of matter." He was one of the earliest experimenters in landscape, genre painting and the nude; everything he touched he touched with reserve and objectivity. In the Arnolfini marriage portrait in London he foretold that precise love of interior detail that two centuries later produced the paintings of Vermeer. The hardness of contour and the uncompromising realism of Jan would seem to be softened in those few works given by modern scholarship to Hubert, where the color is sweeter and more compassionate.

The second of four generations of Flemish masters was dominated by Rogier van der Weyden (1399–1464) and Dieric Bouts, who died in 1475. Rogier was the great tragedian of the Northern Renaissance who endowed his subjects with a spiritual and emotional perfection, a pathos and exaltation, a tenderness and at times a distorted fear which was closer to medieval drama than to medieval art. Born in Tournai he moved to Brussels, where he spent the greater part of his life. He was one of the few Northern artists to go to Italy, where he journeyed for the celebration of the Holy Year in 1450 and presumably saw Fra Angelico at work decorating the private chapel of Pope Nicholas V.

Bouts and Petrus Christus were Hollanders whose work followed closely that of Rogier and the van Eycks. Hugo van der Goes was another giant among the mid-century masters of the sublime and of the commonplace. Paul Fierens has said that "the Flemish led in the conquest of the visible and the invisible, the tangible and the impalpable. To every being and every object, taken in its form and character, they gave its density, its right consistency. To suggest atmosphere they utilized the resources of open air, the delicate nuances of light and shade." Hans Memling (1435–

ADORATION OF THE MAGI—BOSCH

VIRGIN AND CHILD WITH ANGELS
BERNARD VAN ORLEY

PORTRAIT OF A MAN
DIERIC BOUTS

MARIA PORTINARI
MEMLING

PORTRAIT OF A MAN
HUGO VAN DER GOES

A MONASTIC SAINT
PETRUS CHRISTUS

FRANCESCO D'ESTE
ROGIER VAN DER WEYDEN

FLEMISH PORTRAITS, FIFTEENTH CENTURY

MOURNING WOMAN, Mid-15TH CENT.

THE LAMENTATION – PETRUS CHRISTUS

THE BAPTISM – PATINIR

VIRGIN AND ST. JOHN
VAN DER WEYDEN
Philadelphia Museum. Johnson Collection

CHRIST ON THE CROSS
VAN DER WEYDEN
Philadelphia Museum. Johnson Collection

1494) and Gerard David (1460–1523) embodied all the perfections of the school in clarity and sympathy; yet the flawlessness of their finished products reflects a dullness of invention that marks the fleeting moment before the overripe fruit falls from the tree. The last quarter of the century was disturbed by the importations of the Italian Renaissance. The Antwerp "Mannerists," Bosch, Massys, Patinir and van Orley were innovators whose highly individual talents and points of view were to culminate in the popular art of Pieter Bruegel (1525?–1569).

THE HARVESTERS (Detail) – PIETER BRUEGEL (Active 1551, Died 1569)

Bruegel and the Antwerp Mannerists

By 1520 Antwerp had become a teeming commercial capital. Guicciardini, who visited the city, reported that between 100 and 500 ships entered and left it every day. There were 69 master bakers, 78 butchers, 110 barber-surgeons, 594 tailors, and about 300 artists—painters, sculptors, copper engravers and woodcutters. In a memorable passage he describes the frugality of the people and their simple diet of beer and milk, rye bread, cheese and butter, salt pork and fish and many fruits. . . . "They dress well, cleanly and comfortably," he writes, "with sprightly and fantastic fashions. They keep their houses well and furnish them. . . . Marriage feasts last for three days. The groom dresses richly and the bride still more so, and both change every day into new clothes richly and gallantly trimmed. Most of them have the vice of drinking too much, in which they take delight. Sometimes they drink day and night until they injure their bodies, their minds and souls, and doubtless shorten their lives," Their habits Guicciardini condones because of the damp air and adds "they could probably find no means better than wine to dispel the hateful melancholy."

But this "hateful melancholy" was as much a reflection of the times as it was of the damps of the Low Countries, which were divided over the issue of religion. Flanders was Roman Catholic, Holland Protestant.

The fate of Europe had fallen into the hands of the Emperor Charles V, who had inherited the Germanies from his grandfather, the Low Countries from his Burgundian grandmother, and Spain and the New World from his Spanish mother. Through the extraordinary circumstances of his birth the stage was set for the drama of modern European history. It was the age of the Inquisition on the one hand and the scientific discoveries of Keppler and Spinoza on the other. So long as Charles V continued to rule, his natural wisdom and tolerance kept him from precipitating the religious warfare. But his abdication and retirement to a convent in Spain caused him to divide his possessions, giving the German Empire to his brother, and Spain and the Low Countries to his son Philip II. The latter was a zealot and fanatic who, attempting to suppress the Dutch Protestants, set flame to the whole continent.

Bruegel's art stands midway between these warring factions; a professed Lutheran he nevertheless tempered his convictions with a humanity that differed vastly from the humanism of Italy with which his contemporaries in Antwerp were obsessed. Gone was the mystical piety of the fifteenth century; the medieval tradition was broken and Bruegel has remained the father of secular and popular art. "He was the first painter," A. Hyatt Mayor has said, "who saw people as outgrowths of their habit of life. He thus became the ancestor of all painters of character and occupation such as Teniers, Brouwer, Chardin, Millet, and Winslow Homer. He was the first painter who found a satisfying range of drama in life at home or outside his window. By discovering the deepest emotions in everyday events he led the way to Rembrandt."

ST. MICHAEL
Valencian, 15TH CENT.

The Spanish School

SPANISH art has been described as "a singular mélange of mystic exultation and brutal realism, of asceticism and sensualism, of supreme distinction and triviality, of tenderness and ferocity." For Spain was one of the last countries to relinquish its medieval formulae, and Renaissance painting, beginning as late as the sixteenth century, did not come into full growth until the seventeenth. Velázquez, the austere and ascetic Zurbarán, Murillo, a sentimentalist in the best sense of the word, all painters of the later century, were essentially Spanish in their outlook. Of the earlier schools, some were Italianate, others followed the Flemish tradition of Burgundy. While the Spanish prelates of the Inquisition fanatically opposed the luxury and splendor of the papal court at Rome, and required a strict conformance to the old

Bruegel and the Antwerp Mannerists

By 1520 Antwerp had become a teeming commercial capital. Guicciardini, who visited the city, reported that between 100 and 500 ships entered and left it every day. There were 69 master bakers, 78 butchers, 110 barber-surgeons, 594 tailors, and about 300 artists—painters, sculptors, copper engravers and woodcutters. In a memorable passage he describes the frugality of the people and their simple diet of beer and milk, rye bread, cheese and butter, salt pork and fish and many fruits. . . . "They dress well, cleanly and comfortably," he writes, "with sprightly and fantastic fashions. They keep their houses well and furnish them. . . . Marriage feasts last for three days. The groom dresses richly and the bride still more so, and both change every day into new clothes richly and gallantly trimmed. Most of them have the vice of drinking too much, in which they take delight. Sometimes they drink day and night until they injure their bodies, their minds and souls, and doubtless shorten their lives," Their habits Guicciardini condones because of the damp air and adds "they could probably find no means better than wine to dispel the hateful melancholy."

But this "hateful melancholy" was as much a reflection of the times as it was of the damps of the Low Countries, which were divided over the issue of religion. Flanders was Roman Catholic, Holland Protestant.

The fate of Europe had fallen into the hands of the Emperor Charles V, who had inherited the Germanies from his grandfather, the Low Countries from his Burgundian grandmother, and Spain and the New World from his Spanish mother. Through the extraordinary circumstances of his birth the stage was set for the drama of modern European history. It was the age of the Inquisition on the one hand and the scientific discoveries of Keppler and Spinoza on the other. So long as Charles V continued to rule, his natural wisdom and tolerance kept him from precipitating the religious warfare. But his abdication and retirement to a convent in Spain caused him to divide his possessions, giving the German Empire to his brother, and Spain and the Low Countries to his son Philip II. The latter was a zealot and fanatic who, attempting to suppress the Dutch Protestants, set flame to the whole continent.

Bruegel's art stands midway between these warring factions; a professed Lutheran he nevertheless tempered his convictions with a humanity that differed vastly from the humanism of Italy with which his contemporaries in Antwerp were obsessed. Gone was the mystical piety of the fifteenth century; the medieval tradition was broken and Bruegel has remained the father of secular and popular art. "He was the first painter," A. Hyatt Mayor has said, "who saw people as outgrowths of their habit of life. He thus became the ancestor of all painters of character and occupation such as Teniers, Brouwer, Chardin, Millet, and Winslow Homer. He was the first painter who found a satisfying range of drama in life at home or outside his window. By discovering the deepest emotions in everyday events he led the way to Rembrandt."

THE PEASANT WEDDING FEAST (Bride Detail)
Vienna. Kunsthistorisches Museum

CARNIVAL AND LENT (Carnival Detail)
Vienna. Kunsthistorisches Museum

THE ART OF PIETER BRUEGEL

THE WEDDING DANCE (Swing Your Partner Detail)
The Detroit Institute of Art

CARNIVAL AND LENT (Lent Detail)
Vienna. Kunsthistorisches Museum

THE ART OF PIETER BRUEGEL

CHILDREN'S GAMES
Vienna. Kunsthistorisches Museum

THE PROVERB OF THE BIRD THIEF
Vienna. Kunsthistorisches Museum

THE ART OF PIETER BRUEGEL

HARE–ALBRECHT DÜRER, 1471–1528
Vienna. Water Color. (Artext Junior Print 217)

German Art

German art of the Renaissance was tempered by the Reformation, which disapproved the grand style of Papal Rome. The medieval guilds began to lose their corporate identity and the artist was more conscious of his power. He became more objective too, in regard to man and nature and began to study the problems of form and perspective, forsaking religious symbols for realism.

The principal schools of the fifteenth century were those of the Rhineland, of Cologne, which were essentially Gothic, and of the even more mannered school of Westphalia. At the end of the century appeared the two outstanding personalities of German art, Albrecht Dürer of Nuremburg and Hans Holbein the Younger, who settled in Basel. Dürer brought to Germany a draughtsmanship of surpassing sweep and power and, through his Italian schooling, a sense of monumental decoration. These qualities together with great natural gifts he handed on to his followers. Grünewald, the Cranachs and Holbein. The eminent humanist, Erasmus, attracted Holbein to the English court of the Tudor monarch Henry VIII. In Germany his influence counted for a masterly understanding of composition that gathered together the knowledge of his predecessors, and for accuracy in rendering materials, no less than in analyzing character. His portraits, and those of Dürer, approached life from opposite directions. To Dürer, life was filled with human tragedy, with thwarted hopes and the sense of impending dissolution, from which there was salvation only in redemption. Holbein, housed in the luxury of the English court, viewed life as a glittering pageant.

ANNO.1532. ÆTATIS·SVÆ·29

A MEMBER OF THE WEDIGH FAMILY
HANS HOLBEIN THE YOUNGER

Painted in London in 1532 in the Steelyard or quarter of the German merchants.
The Renaissance in England was exclusively an art of importation that con-
cerned itself with adapting Italian principles to flamboyant Gothic architecture
—really a problem of grafting a southern style upon a northern climate. In
painting, except for a few imitators of Holbein, little was accomplished.

HENRY FREDERICK PRINCE OF WALES
UNKNOWN ENGLISH PAINTER

*This detail of a picture showing the Prince with Sir John Harrington is dated
1603. It is characteristic of the style of English miniature painters in Elizabethan and Jacobean times. Here we see that marriage of French and Flemish
traits which developed in the School of Fontainebleau and was transported by
the Stuarts to the English Court.*

THE JUDGMENT OF PARIS (Detail) – LUCAS CRANACH

HIERONYMUS HOLZSCHUHER–DÜRER
Berlin. Collection of the Kaiser Friedrich Museum

DEATH ON HORSEBACK, Bronze–German

ST. MICHAEL
Valencian, 15TH CENT.

The Spanish School

SPANISH art has been described as "a singular mélange of mystic exultation and brutal realism, of asceticism and sensualism, of supreme distinction and triviality, of tenderness and ferocity." For Spain was one of the last countries to relinquish its medieval formulae, and Renaissance painting, beginning as late as the sixteenth century, did not come into full growth until the seventeenth. Velázquez, the austere and ascetic Zurbarán, Murillo, a sentimentalist in the best sense of the word, all painters of the later century, were essentially Spanish in their outlook. Of the earlier schools, some were Italianate, others followed the Flemish tradition of Burgundy. While the Spanish prelates of the Inquisition fanatically opposed the luxury and splendor of the papal court at Rome, and required a strict conformance to the old

116   **FIFTY CENTURIES OF ART**

CHRIST DRIVING MONEY CHANGERS FROM THE TEMPLE–EL GRECO
Minneapolis Institute of Arts

dogmas and iconography, their admiration for Michelangelo and Raphael nevertheless crept into the work of the court painters. Madrid received an influx of Venetian painting, too, after the coronation in 1530 of Charles V as Emperor of the Holy Roman Empire at Bologna where he was painted by Titian. The influence of Venice seemed to dominate the art of the Spanish capital; and out of this milieu arose Domenico Theotokopoulos, called El Greco, a Cretan by birth who studied in Venice in Titian's studio and finally settled after 1580 in Toledo in Spain. Following at first the tenets of the Venetian School, El Greco developed a manner that was suffused with a wholly Spanish mysticism to which he brought a mind delighting in music, tossed by spiritual emotion. In his disproportionately long and twisted figures that flout the most elementary rules of anatomy, in his intense bloodless portraits, in the undulating vertical lines and contrasting use of black and white there is a "trembling elevation of prayer and ecstasy, an impoverished ascetic will and a marvelous melody sustained by a harmony resembling a night sky broken by violet tinted clouds, silvery pallors, pale yellows and green lights." The *View of Toledo* shows the passion and at the same time the restraint which were characteristic of his ability to create mood in landscapes.

El Greco's intense spiritual and rebellious curiosity was reflected in the perfect and supremely elegant art of Velázquez (1599–1660), who applied himself to the more classic formulae of the Venetians without abandoning himself to the violent distortions of El Greco. The aristocratic isolation of the Spanish temperament, apparent in his deeply psychological portraits, the pride even of the beggar, the sense of *el honor*

VIEW OF TOLEDO—EL GRECO (1541-1614)

"It is the only one of his paintings which can be called a land-
scape. In it his intention was not to paint the city as it actually
appears, but to present its essence or spirit, even though that
demanded some rearrangement of the buildings shrinking be-
neath the turbulent threatening clouds."

that appears consistently in Spanish literature from the *Cid* to *Don Quixote* were
brought out by Velázquez and his immediate contemporaries and successors. Herrera,
Murillo, Ribera, and Zurbarán.

Spanish painting thereafter suffered a decline until there appeared in the latter
part of the eighteenth century a revolutionary equally as important as El Greco—
Goya—one of the outstanding geniuses of Spanish painting. Because of his qualities
of lyric gaiety and comic verve, pathos and satire, Goya even more than Velázquez
was the counterpart of Cervantes. At times a madman and a libertine who frequently
reached moments of extraordinary religious heights, Goya excelled as a portraitist
because of his amazing insight into human character. No artist had a greater influence
on Manet and the French Impressionists, who adopted the violent contrasts of Goya's
palette and the vividness of his color.

CARDINAL NIÑO DE GUEVARA – EL GRECO

THE SURRENDER OF BREDA – VELÁZQUEZ
Madrid. The Prado

POPE INNOCENT X–VELÁZQUEZ
Rome. The Doria Palace

LAS MENINAS–VELÁZQUEZ
Madrid. The Prado (Artext Junior Print 285)

THE CONDE–DUQUE DE OLIVARES–VELÁZQUEZ

*This great equestrian portrait of the Spanish "Scourge of the Netherlands"
has recently been acquired by the Metropolitan from the Earl of Elgin.*

ANNUNCIATION–ZURBARAN
Philadelphia Museum of Art

MADONNA–MURILLO (1618–1682)
The Metropolitan Museum of Art

THE SPANISH SCHOOL

CHRIST AMONG THE DOCTORS—RIBERA (1591–1652)
Vienna. Kunsthistorisches Museum

DON MANUEL OSORIO—GOYA (1745–1828)
The Metropolitan Museum of Art

THE SPANISH SCHOOL

THE FAMILY OF CHARLES IV
Madrid. The Prado

RIOTERS
Madrid. The Prado

THE ART OF GOYA

BLINDMAN'S BUFF
Madrid. The Prado

BULLFIGHT—GOYA
The Metropolitan Museum of Art

THE ART OF GOYA

VENUS AND ADONIS—PETER PAUL RUBENS

This picture was given by the Austrian Emperor to the Duke of Marlborough
for the gallery at Blenheim Palace. The head of Adonis was restored by Romney.

Reformation and Catholic Reaction

THE art which had developed in Flanders was an art of realism as distinguished from the idealistic art of Italy and the negative mysticism of Spain. In Italy, man was seen created in the image of God, and his God-like quality was emphasized. Flemish art was homelier. The saints and holy men of the van Eycks, of van der Goes, van der Weyden and Memling were taken from the simple, patient, plain types of the country. But through the sincerity of their vision and the triumphant skill of their execution these early painters endowed the prosaic with a nobility which, per-haps less radiant than the Italian, was no less intense. Italian culture had crossed the

Alps and was brought to the Low Countries by artists who themselves had visited the centers of Italy or in some other way had learned to know Italian art. As the Italian influence became more pronounced, the human body was pictured as more beautiful. Paintings were grander in scale and more suave in execution.

The climax of this movement is reached in the painting of Peter Paul Rubens (1577–1640) and his follower Anthony van Dyck (1599–1641). These two figures dominated the Low Countries throughout the Thirty Years' War; their influence, particularly that of the former, being felt all over Europe. Rubens, courtier, ambassador of the Spanish Netherlands, court painter to the Regent, to the Kings of Spain, France and England, was the teacher of nearly every Flemish painter of the seventeenth century; he was stirred chiefly by Michelangelo and the Venetians, expressing the abundance of his genius in great cycles of historical, mythological and religious murals where it was possible to exclude everything of a genre character in favor of the heroic interpretation of the human animal. Twice married, first to Isabella Brandt and after her death to Hélène Fourment, Rubens lived a life of opulence and luxury, showering his affections upon the persons and things he loved. He made the human form the fundamental motif of his art, giving it an overflowing vitality that even in old age had a certain youthful elasticity. By divesting the people in his pictures of their everyday clothes and giving them a mythical nudity, he united man with nature and was thus able to carry out with the assistance of his large crew the bombastic allegories which cover the walls of so many European palaces. His wonderful sense of color, his titanic individuality, and his joy of life enabled him to be the unique assembler and innovator of his time. Very often he was carried away by the sheer impact of his own ideas and it is therefore in his smaller sketches that we see the artist at his best. Van Dyck, lacking his master's exuberant vitality, developed a refinement and elegance which won him the position of court painter to Charles I where he exerted an enormous influence on the English School.

The liberation of Holland by the Princes of Orange from the domination of Spain and the Roman Catholic Church brought about a rapid artistic development which thrived upon the Dutch genius for genre painting. Even greater realists than the early Flemish, the Dutchmen, no longer subject to the demands of the Church, "turned to the task of painting the portrait of the nation" which they performed in minute and happy easel pictures for which there was a great demand on the part of the wealthy, home-loving burghers. Intimate domestic scenes, still-lifes, animal pictures, landscapes, everything in which the eye could find color and order, were transformed into small pictures that adorned the walls of their tall narrow houses. Accurate transcription of the visible world was their ideal, but different from the mystical realism of Flanders, the Dutch realism was a sociable realism. It relinquished the heroic heightening of effect so characteristic in Rubens, and paid homage to a simple, but lighter exuberance, already seen in the art of Bruegel. Trial and tribulation are banned, and instead we find a passion for detail and for the gayer aspects of the idle hour and the holiday.

THE TRIUMPHAL ENTRY OF HENRY IV INTO PARIS—RUBENS

A sketch for the mural decorations at the Louvre.

Festivals in which supreme discretion and riotous license are at opposite poles, scenes so interesting to the Flemish moralist, are supplanted by the more peaceful arts of husbandry and the pleasures of the table. People converse and play in houses, and are seen moving about the streets and in churches. From these scenes was developed an architectural city landscape that is quite unique.

The problem of light, because of the soft changing skies above the Netherlands, was the chief lesson of the Dutch painters, particularly of Rembrandt van Rijn (1606–1669), the greatest master of light and shade that Europe has ever known. Light over the landscape at different hours of the day, during the changing seasons, sunshine and dusk; light upon the gnarled and knotted oak tree in the forest, or on the limitless space above the flat inviting plains, dotted with villages and cities, affected the Dutchman as a spiritual experience. To Rembrandt, who absorbed this placid Dutch life and who interested himself in the philosophical problems of man's relation to his environment, chiaroscuro was essential to the differentiation of planes and the merging of the background with the foreground. Rembrandt is at once the simplest and the most complex personality in the history of art. He knew great success and abysmal failure, extravagant riches and the direst poverty. He was the poet of the ghetto and one of the most prolific illustrators of the Bible ever known, breaking away from the pictorial tradition of the Middle Ages to portray religious emotions and experiences in everyday terms. He was a naturalist who defied the ordinary laws of naturalism which characterize his early works, to become at the end of his life the

LUCAS VAN UFFEL - VAN DYCK

PORTRAIT OF A LADY - VAN DYCK

greatest impressionist of all time. Always it was light and its effect upon personalities and circumstances, on human life and environment, that absorbed his interest; "he plunged his world into a bath of gold."

In contrast with the overpowering scale of figures in the foreground of Flemish pictures, in Dutch landscapes they are small and conduct themselves with a quietude and impersonality reminiscent of Chinese landscape. The colors are controlled by a golden tone through which the sunlight penetrates or recedes according to the mood of the canvas.

Because of the gigantic achievement of Rembrandt, not only in landscape, but in religious themes and portraiture, the Dutch masters have suffered by comparison. Frans Hals had the gift of penetrating vision to a greater degree than any of his countrymen, but there were many other able portraitists, some of whose works are illustrated in the following pages.

The constant threat of the sea is ever present in Dutch painting; witness their touching belief in the safety of the dykes, the winding canals through fertile fields and tortuous brick canyons weaving through spotless cities. Jan Vermeer of Delft, whose painting of his native city in the Mauritshuis leads the list of these intimate city water-scapes, was also the master of the interior, in which he created a different, less turbulent effect of light than Rembrandt, influencing the art of Metsu, Terborch, and Pieter de Hooch, painters whose portraits are as much of places as they are of people. Van Goyen, Cuyp, Hobbema, Salomon and Jacob Ruisdael, each one offered some unique aspect of the Hollander's idea of landscape in which animals and flowers played such an important role. It was perhaps this emphasis upon the contemplative life which gave rise by contrast to the rowdy boisterous tavern scenes by Brouwer, van Ostade, and Jan Steen.

THE ARTIST AND ISABELLA BRANT–RUBENS
Munich. Ältere Pinakothek

JACOB AND LABAN–VICTORS, DUTCH

PORTRAIT OF THE ARTIST—REMBRANDT

THE TOILET OF BATHSHEBA—REMBRANDT

SIMEON IN THE TEMPLE—REMBRANDT
The Hague. Mauritshuis

FLORA—REMBRANDT

THE NIGHT WATCH—REMBRANDT
Amsterdam. Rijksmuseum

JAN SIX—REMBRANDT
Amsterdam. Jan Six Museum

THE ARTIST IN HIS STUDIO
Vienna. Kunsthistorisches Museum

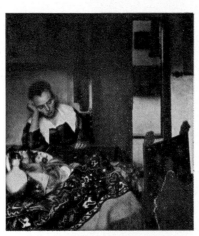

GIRL ASLEEP
The Metropolitan Museum of Art

LADY WITH A LUTE
The Metropolitan Museum of Art

THE ART OF VERMEER

HEAD OF A YOUNG GIRL
The Hague. Mauritshuis

VIEW OF DELFT
The Hague. Mauritshuis

THE ART OF VERMEER

WOMAN WITH WATER JUG – VERMEER
The Metropolitan Museum of Art

THE BOUQUET – AMBROSIUS BOSSCHAERT
The Hague. Mauritshuis

MALLE BABBE–HALS
(1580–1666)

LADY PLAYING THEORBO–TERBORCH
(1617–1681)

A MERRY COMPANY–JAN STEFN
The Hague. Mauritshuis

A FAMILY GROUP—P. DE HOOCH (1629–1683)
Vienna. Kunsthistorisches Museum

PORTRAIT OF A MAN
FRANS HALS (1580–1666)

QUAY AT LEYDEN–VAN DER HEYDEN
(1637–1712)

SKATING–BEERSTRAATEN
(1622–1666)

FLOWERS–RACHEL RUYS
(1664–1750)

GRAINFIELDS–JACOB VAN RUYSDAEL
(1628–1682)

YOUNG HERDSMEN WITH COWS–CUYP
(1620–1691)

THE DUTCH SCHOOL

VESPERS OF THE HOLY GHOST AND VIEW OF PARIS

Jean Fouquet executed this miniature for the celebrated Book of Hours of Étienne Chevalier about 1460 when Enguerrand Charenton(?) was painting the pathetic Pietà, now in the Louvre, for the convent at Villeneuve-les-Avignon. (Opposite.) Both of these works epitomize that last flourish of Gothic art under Louis XI before the Italian Renaissance was introduced to France through the campaigns of Charles VIII and Louis XII. New York. Robert Lehman Collection.

THE "AVIGNON PIETÀ"—French c. 1460

The French Tradition

Francis I came to the throne in 1515 and summoned to his court at Fontaine-bleau Leonardo da Vinci, Andrea del Sarto, Primaticcio and the goldsmith Benvenuto Cellini. The style of the Florentine High Renaissance was adopted and refined by such architects and sculptors as Jean Goujon and Pierre Bontemps. While the marriage of Francis' son, Henri II, to Catherine de Medici had established the Renaissance as the court style, the Italianizing influence was in some measure balanced by that of men like the Clouets, who continued to paint in the Flemish tradition.

After the foundation of the Académie Française by Cardinal Richelieu in the reign of Louis XIII, and of the École des Beaux-Arts by Louis XIV, France became more and more consciously classical. In art, in literature, in music as well as in religion, *le grand siècle* reflected the rigid absolutism of the monarchical idea which domi-

SUSANNE DE BOURBON–MASTER OF MOULINS
New York. Robert Lehman Collection

nated the politics of Europe after 1600. Painting developed a cold intellectual attitude
evident in the works of the court painters at Versailles; Le Brun, Rigaud and their
followers turned out routine commissions in great profusion, while Poussin and Claude
Lorrain modified and enriched the art by giving it a formal classic color and composition. Poussin lived many years in Rome and was enthralled by classical antiquity; he
was obsessed with the truths of history and the expression of the sentiments aroused by
historic circumstance. His inspirations were not only antiquity itself but the Old
Testament and the Gospels. He read the texts thoroughly and put them into action by
posing his models in arrangements of drapery and noble architecture. He was, perhaps,
less a creator than a stage manager; the only nature which he tolerated was mythological and historical. He was the embodiment in paint of the classic dramatists, Cor-
neille, Racine and Molière. Claude Lorrain was less formal, the painter of sun and
sunlight. Also schooled in Rome, he was fascinated by the romance of sunsets in which
antique ruins are placed against the skyline with idyllic shepherds and shepherdesses
evoking bucolic poetry. These men with their lesser followers and imitators were all

CHARLES IX – FRANÇOIS CLOUET
Vienna. Kunsthistorisches Museum

in the service of the King and employed in the task of creating the great monument of his reign, the Palace of Versailles.

With the death of Louis XIV in 1715 French art, particularly of the court, gave itself up to gallantry and lightness, more in keeping with the gay morals and fashions of the times. To meet this indulgence and elegance the Baroque style, which had been characterized by a movement of silhouette—that is to say, a wild almost centrifugal abandon of the figure from the compact and natural repose of the Renaissance classical ideal—was transformed to a graceful movement of surface and texture in the Rococo. This change of surface is even more marked in the sculpture of Pajou, and Houdon than in the sophisticated and charmingly executed paintings of Fragonard, Watteau and Boucher. Portraiture flourished steadily until the Revolution although it suffered from the decadence of the Rococo tradition. Chardin, whose reputation is primarily as a master of still life, also departed from the pattern and devoted himself to the things which he saw with his own eyes. His solidity and strength offer a marked contrast to the graceful brilliance of his contemporaries under Louis XV and Louis XVI.

TRIUMPH OF NEPTUNE AND AMPHITRITE–POUSSIN (1594–1665)

This picture which embodies the classicist spirit of the grand siècle was commissioned by Cardinal Richelieu and later was owned by Catherine the Great of Russia. Philadelphia Museum.

FLIGHT INTO EGYPT–CLAUDE LORRAIN (1600?–1682)
Dresden. State Gallery. (Artext Junior Print 265)

LE MEZZETIN - WATTEAU
(1684–1721)

LOVE LETTER - FRAGONARD
(1732–1806)

THE HOUSE OF CARDS—CHARDIN (1699–1779)
Washington. The National Gallery of Art, Mellon Collection

THE GRAHAM CHILDREN—WILLIAM HOGARTH
London. The Tate Gallery

The British School

THE art of painting was longer in maturing in the British Isles than on the continent. Beginning with the Renaissance, it was primarily an art of importation—foreign artists such as Holbein, van Dyck, Lely and Kneller, who were attached to the English court. A sturdy tradition of arts and crafts had been maintained under the Tudors and in the reign of Queen Elizabeth, but compared with the state of the arts across the Channel, provincialism and usefulness were the order of the day; England excelled in furniture and the household arts while contributing little in painting and sculpture. This was not due to lack of talent or artistic enterprise so much as it was to political circumstances. Strong in architecture, sculpture and miniature painting in early Gothic times, the individuality of English art steadily declined and became more and more imitative of the French until finally the Wars of the Roses, and the Hundred Years War with its frequent transference of the court to Normandy, had completely merged its character with the international style of the Northern Renaissance. The Stuarts were, to be sure, great collectors seeking to emulate the France of

THE TRAGIC MUSE—REYNOLDS
San Marino, California. The Henry E. Huntington Library

Richelieu and Mazarin; Charles I, Lord Arundel, and the Duke of Buckingham having amassed the most splendid treasures from Italy and the Low Countries. But this activity came to an abrupt end with Cromwell and the Commonwealth. Between the execution of Charles I in 1649 and the Restoration in 1688 there was virtually no creative art in sculpture or painting in England.

The Protectorate passed; the Court returned and life became more placid. English society of the Restoration, with its gallantry, its comedy of manners and general air of distinction, gave rise to a school of portraiture which for elegance and grace, charm and wholesome freshness, was unrivaled. William Hogarth (1697–1764), often referred to as the founder of the British School, was still Cromwellian in his point of view, employing his talent for tractarian and moralistic purposes. The series of paintings such as *The Rake's Progress*, made so popular by the inexpensive engravings of the pictures, in which he pointed out the sins of the age, were his most famous works. His portraits tell us all there is to know about the sitters, yet frequently the power of his expression is softened with humor and sympathy.

"PINKIE"–SIR THOMAS LAWRENCE
San Marino, California. The Henry E. Huntington Library

Sir Joshua Reynolds, the founder and first president of the Royal Academy, was the teacher and acknowledged leader of his contemporaries, giving a prestige to the artistic career hitherto unknown in England. His scholarship far exceeded his imagination, and his portraits, like his famous *Discourses*, resound with the ponderous rhetoric of his good friend Dr. Johnson. He profoundly admired the Italians of the High Renaissance and what he lacked in taste he supplied in intellectual vision. *Mrs. Siddons as The Tragic Muse* has the grandeur and heroism of England's Augustan Age; it is the epitome of the period portrait. Thomas Gainsborough (1727–1788) is the glass of fashion reflecting the spontaneity and brilliance of Mayfair and Bath. No painter has ever caught so well as he the implications of aristocratic society, the snobbery of the Georgian country house and the utterly unself-conscious acceptance of great wealth, so characteristic of the English upper classes throughout the eighteenth and nineteenth centuries. These were, indeed, England's centuries and both the vitality and arrogance are qualities familiar in our own colonial heritage. Fair play, the innocence of childhood, the manly Anglo-Saxon virtues, together with the ethereal idealism of the poets of the Lake Country, are given full expression in Gainsborough's

"BLUE BOY"–THOMAS GAINSBOROUGH
San Marino, California. The Henry E. Huntington Library

Blue Boy and in the equally celebrated *Pinkie* by Sir Thomas Lawrence (1769–1830). Portraiture declined during the Regency; the charm and sweetness are still there in the works of Beechey and Opie. Romney and Hoppner continued the fashionable portrait; only in Scotland with Raeburn does a more serious realism appear.

As portraiture declined, the art of landscape painting waxed stronger and it was in the English experiments in the field in the late eighteenth and early nineteenth centuries that the Barbizon and Impressionist schools found many of their ideas. It was a subject admirably suited to the British temperament, particularly that of the country gentleman; a well-ordered landscape, a private park in which animals and human beings appear quite as a matter of course according to their stations in life, a happy, thoroughly unintellectual appreciation of nature. A more serious attempt to understand nature followed in the works of John Constable, who never sought more romantic or grander subjects than the pleasant rural scenes about him. He did away with the dark brown, "old violin tones," and introduced into landscape painting the true colors of nature. It is in the versatility of Turner that one sees the culmination of the English sense of landscape in the nineteenth century.

LORD ROBERTSON – RAEBURN

GRAND CANAL, VENICE – TURNER

THE BELL INN – MORLAND

VIEW ON THE STOUR NEAR DEDHAM – CONSTABLE

THE ENGLISH SCHOOL (18TH CENT.)

French Painting:
The Modern Movement

THE Modern Movement which was centered primarily in France is the child of revolution, of the fall of the Bastille and the Industrial Revolution of Manchester and Birmingham. The nineteenth century had witnessed changes as important for the arts as they were for politics and the social sciences. With its canons of beauty and proportion, its arbitrary standards of line and composition, the ideal of the Academy was superseded by a new ideal. Instead of the color harmony and golden tone of the Italian Renaissance, a new individuality and realism became popular. It was an age of reason and of scientific discovery in which the problem of light absorbed the attention of both painter and physicist. The former turned to landscape, where he had opportunity to study in natural color the effect of sunlight and shadow, while the latter developed the science of photography, an invention which was to produce radical changes in the theory of vision and in the problems of reality.

Furthermore, the opening of the Grand Gallery of the Louvre, where artists for the first time were freely permitted to study the works of the great masters, had exerted an enormous influence. Instead of developing an eclecticism composed of Dutch, Italian and Spanish elements, they discovered there revolutionary techniques: the basic new laws of composition, the objective representation of actual things, the "significance of form" and how it may be achieved by pure color; all these qualities the younger generation learned, together with a new taste for subject matter.

As the century wore on it became more and more apparent that the battle of modern painting was to be waged between the exterior visual world of fact and the abstract, subjective inner world of the intelligence. Since the early Renaissance, painting had become definitely pictorial; the decorative effect was, except in the cases of a few isolated geniuses, subordinated to the recording of historic fact, either in the form of portraiture or as the illustration of important events. But the commercial possibilities of the steel engraving and the rapid progress of photography relieved the artist of the external pressure of official pictures and left him greater opportunity

THE DEATH OF SOCRATES (Detail) – JACQUES-LOUIS DAVID (1748–1825)

MLLE. DU VAL D'OGNE – DAVID OR FOLLOWER

FRANÇOIS MARIUS GRANET – INGRES (1780–1867)
Aix-en-Provence. Le Musée Granet

ODALISQUE IN GRAY–INGRES

ABDUCTION OF REBECCA–DELACROIX

AUTUMN–MILLET

THIRD CLASS CARRIAGE–DAUMIER

THIRD CLASS CARRIAGE (Detail)–HONORÉ DAUMIER (1808–1879)

to inject his own personality into his work. In the hundred years following the French Revolution there appeared therefore more individual styles in painting than had been known in the five thousand years of the history of art. It is thus impossible to consider the nineteenth century in terms of schools or academies. It was a thoroughly individualistic performance. While it is true that there were certain definite movements, such as that at Barbizon for landscape, the classicism of David and Ingres, the conflicting poles of romanticism and realism, and the later Impressionists, these movements were merely theories of painting to which the several artists subscribed with greater or fewer reservations according to their temperaments. They were no longer the simple craftsmen of the Middle Ages but had become complex personalities in a still more complex modern world.

GIPSY GIRL AT THE FOUNTAIN—COROT
Philadelphia Museum of Art

VETHEUIL—CLAUDE MONET (1840–1926)

BATHER IN THE WOODS—PISSARRO (1830–1903)

Victor Hugo's *Manifesto* in 1827 inaugurated the program of romanticism in literature in which the arts soon took an equal share. The Romanticists, of whom Delacroix was to be the chief exponent in painting, were called upon to choose between the accumulated culture of the past and the apparent barrenness of a materialistic future—very much the dilemma that the artist claims to feel today in the choice of subject matter. But Delacroix's greatness lay in carrying on the coloristic reform which, started by Goya, had freed French art from the clutches of Classicism. The men of Barbizon, Millet, Diaz and their followers, devoted themselves to the same purpose but avoided Delacroix's stories of medieval passion and the hot glamour of Algeria.

BOATING—MANET (1832–1883)

LADIES OF THE VILLAGE—COURBET (1819–1877)

JAMES TISSOT—EDGAR DEGAS (1834–1917)

WOMAN WITH CHRYSANTHEMUMS—EDGAR DEGAS

TORERO SALUTING—ÉDOUARD MANET (1832–1883)

LE FOYER—EDGAR DEGAS

THE BATHERS—RENOIR (1841–1920)
Philadelphia. Carroll S. Tyson Collection

BAL À BOUGIVAL—RENOIR
Boston. Museum of Fine Arts

MADAME CHARPENTIER AND CHILDREN–RENOIR

Daumier was in a sense the first modern artist of the French School in that he left to photography the accurate representation of the material world and applied himself to the characterization of the inner spirit. He excelled in the art of caricature, giving it a monumental and functional intensity. Courbet and Corot were realists but with a classic bias, the latter occupying the relation to the new school of landscape that existed between Delacroix and Ingres. Courbet was essentially a painter's painter, a great technician, a man of fearless political independence whose irrepressible talent made up for his occasional lapses of taste.

In 1864 the Impressionist Movement was instigated by Édouard Manet and Claude Monet who, to accomplish coloristic reforms, moved their easels to the open air where they might better study light and atmosphere. Although the Barbizon painters had done this to some extent, they still clung to the official traditions of heavy, dark tones. Theirs was an "effort to enrich painting psychologically and to widen space physically." Manet believed that nature must reveal itself without embellishment or flattery and that color must be in accordance with the laws of natural light. Thus in painting the countryside about Paris in its infinite variety of delicate nuances, Manet reversed the practice of Corot, who had returned to the earlier method of painting nature not as she is, but according to the classical ideal. Claude Monet, Pissarro, and Sisley merely enlarged upon the possibilities of Manet's *plein air* method. It was left to Renoir to bathe the painting of the Impressionists with a wonderful pagan

IA ORANA MARIA – PAUL GAUGUIN (1848–1903)

hedonism, which he achieved by the rotation of warm and cool tones to an extent that had not been accomplished by any painter since El Greco. It was another early Impressionist, Cézanne, a former pupil of Pissarro, who discovered the weakness of the impressionistic formula, its lack of solidity and design. To use his own words, he determined to give this art "the solidity and enduring quality of ancient art—of the art of the museums." Opposing Manet's program of naturalistic color (which tends to absorption), he substituted a method whereby color used in successive planes would project form from the canvas. He produced landscapes, still-lifes and figures, interiors and portraits of a rare beauty, in which the perception of color is incredibly sensitive and profound. Edgar Degas, whose passion for the ballet and gifts for portraiture produced many of the most exquisite paintings of the period, marks the culmination of the Impressionist Movement—a link between the classical tradition and the modern world. Gauguin, van Gogh, Seurat and Toulouse-Lautrec carried forward the experiments of the Impressionists, each concentrating upon the impact of his own personality; Gauguin, who opened up the exotic possibilities of the South Seas, was the Pierre

162   **FIFTY CENTURIES OF ART**

POSTER–TOULOUSE-LAUTREC (1864–1901)

Loti or Lafcadio Hearn of painting. Seurat and Signac experimented with breaking up the colors of the spectrum into a system of dots known as pointillism. Lautrec was the poet of the café and dance halls of Montmartre, and Vincent van Gogh revealed through his violent vibrations of color the madness and inner conflict that ended in his suicide. These artists, so different from one another, universally recognized that all individual forms contained within a picture could never be completely homogeneous until the element of time (which is inherent in optical naturalism), was removed and the idea of simultaneous action and rhythmic composition fully understood. The problem of the past fifty years has been, indeed, the interpenetration of time and space. Proceeding by the reduction of modeling and by the use of complementary tones, they arrived at a more or less flat juxtaposition of color forms in preparation for the relatively pure abstractions of Matisse and Picasso.

During the early years of the twentieth century this intellectualism ran its course. Les Fauves, a group in Paris, revolted in 1906 against the naturalism of the Impressionists and substituted for it a new palette based upon a formal abstract study of archaeology. Revolutionists in color, they borrowed many methods of stylization from the Egyptian and the Byzantine and other archaic periods. Then followed the

PORTRAIT OF THE ARTIST
Collection of Vincent W. van Gogh

LA BERCEUSE
Amsterdam, Municipal Museum

VAN GOGH'S BEDROOM IN ARLES
Collection of Vincent W. van Gogh

CYPRESSES
The Metropolitan Museum of Art

IRISES
Collection of Vincent W. van Gogh

THE ART OF VAN GOGH

L'ARLÉSIENNE (Detail) – VINCENT VAN GOGH (1853–1890)
The Metropolitan Museum of Art

THE GULF OF MARSEILLES SEEN FROM L'ESTAQUE

STILL LIFE: APPLES AND PRIMROSES

THE ART OF PAUL CÉZANNE (1839–1906)

STUDY FOR LA GRANDE JATTE (Detail) – GEORGES SEURAT (1859–1891)

PORTRAIT OF GERTRUDE STEIN—PICASSO
Bequeathed by Gertrude Stein to the Metropolitan Museum

WHITE PLUMES—MATISSE
Minneapolis Institute of Art. (Artext Junior Print 170)

STILL LIFE, MANDOLIN—BRAQUE
Private Collection (Artext Junior Print 409)

LE GOURMET—PICASSO
New York. Chester Dale Collection (Artext Junior Print 437)

NUDE DESCENDING THE STAIR CASE—MARCEL DUCHAMP
Philadelphia Museum of Art. Signed and dated 1912

scientific movement of the Cubists, who made no attempt to organize nature but tried to produce works that were intrinsically beautiful without aid or setting. The beauty of the object existed for them only in the eye of the beholder. With the First World War the artist's hopes for a scientific world of art were shattered. Attempted reorganizations of his thoughts followed with breathless succession; Futurists, Symbolists, Expressionists, Synthesists, Intimists, Orphists, and Purists. The emphasis on the subjective in the later works of the Dadaists and Surrealists has led, quite logically, to the more sterile abstractions of the mid-twentieth century in which the artist, overwhelmed by the scientific progress of the world in which he lives, is determined to assert his own individual personality by rejecting the accumulations of the art of the past for his private selections from the world of the present. Thus we see exhibited the most intimate commentaries on modern invention, communications, electronics, the airplane and the phenomena of psychological investigation. While this has produced many exceptional talents, the great majority of contemporary artists are merely marking time in their continuous self-searching for new forms. The artist has more to

FIFTY CENTURIES OF ART

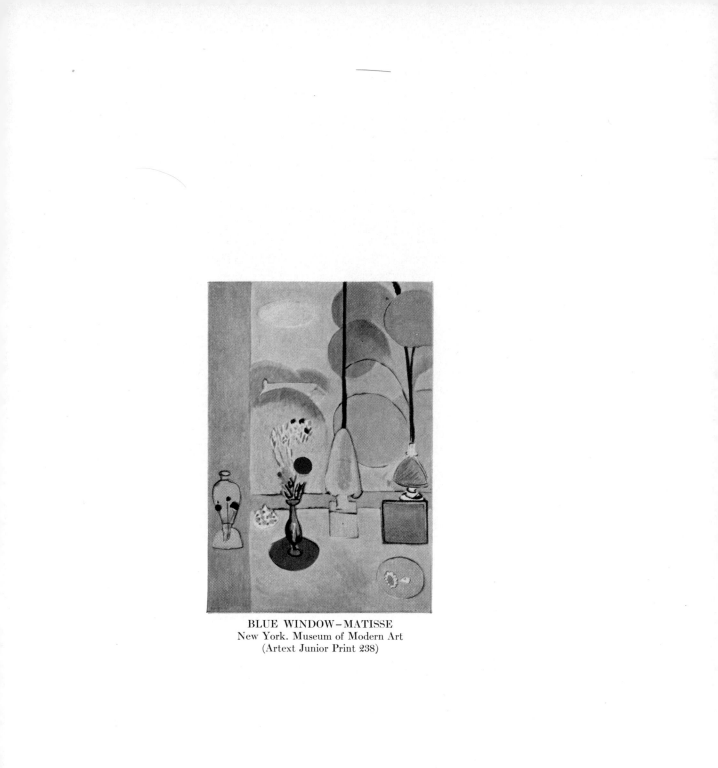

BLUE WINDOW—MATISSE
New York. Museum of Modern Art
(Artext Junior Print 238)

select from today than he ever had before. Time alone will tell whether or not the individual artist can rise above his limited personal experiences and again apply his talents to the expression of those universal aspirations which throughout the ages have made him the servant of religion and humanity.

HENRY GIBBS–AMERICAN c. 1670
From a private collection

MRS. BOURNE–COPLEY
(1737–1815)

GEORGE WASHINGTON–TRUMBULL
(1756–1803)

The leopard with the harmless kid laid down.
And not one savage beast was seen to frown.

The wolf did with the lambkin dwell in peace.
His grim carniv'rous nature there did cease.

The lion with the fatling on did move,
A little child was leading them in love.

When the great PENN his famous treaty made,
With indian chiefs beneath the elm-trees shade.

PEACEABLE KINGDOM—EDWARD HICKS
Cooperstown. New York State Historical Society

American Art

AN EPILOGUE TO EUROPE

AMONG the early colonists portraiture arose as a matter of record to gratify the vanity of wealthy men and to preserve the features of distinguished ones. "Limners" or "face painters," carriage and house painters were called upon in many instances to supply the need where a more sophisticated artisan was lacking. Before 1750 the face painters, exhibiting scant talent, were scarcely to be compared with European portrait painters of the same period; but by the middle of the eighteenth century our colonial face painting began to have a more standardized and professional look. John Singleton Copley was the first American to achieve even a modest standing in the general history of art. His pre-eminence among his contemporaries depended not so much on any innovation as on his increased powers of observation and an ability to state uncompromisingly what he saw.

Benjamin West was the first American to acquire European prestige. Born in Pennsylvania, a Quaker, he died in London in 1820, where he finished his career as

WASHINGTON–GILBERT STUART

QUEEN VICTORIA–THOMAS SULLY

THE AMERICAN SCHOOL–MATTHEW PRATT

THE PRODIGAL SON–BENJAMIN WEST

STAIRCASE GROUP–C. W. PEALE
Philadelphia Museum of Art

THE AMERICAN SCHOOL

president of the Royal Academy. He had studied in Italy and produced a series of mythological and historical canvases executed in the bombastic and grandiose manner of Sir Joshua. Gilbert Stuart of Rhode Island was the ablest American portrait painter of his day and has hardly been surpassed in this country since. Matthew Pratt (1734–1805), Charles Willson Peale and his sons were equally able practitioners, deriving their knowledge of limning from West's studio in London at which they all studied. John Trumbull (1756–1843) was the historical painter of Connecticut. It was left to Thomas Sully, who lived until 1872, to close the portrait tradition of the early Republic.

During and following the War of Independence political developments had been uppermost in the minds of most Americans and young painters executed rhetorical paintings of battles and portraits of the nation's heroes. Still English in tradition, though independent in government, America continued to follow British artistic standards although there was lacking in the new country much of the pleasant life of elegance that gave the works of Reynolds and Gainsborough such an aristocratic hallmark. The subject matter of the Royal Academy, the Bible, the ancient poets, contemporary history, continued to engross the late work of West, while a romantic tendency appeared in the work of the painter-inventor, Samuel F. B. Morse and Washington Allston.

The Hudson River School represented the first break from the English tradition and an attempt to found an American art, but the heroic landscape painters did not rise above the level of their age.

Within a period of fifteen years after the Civil War, American art had been lifted out of the provincial stage by a remarkable group of painters; Winslow Homer and Thomas Eakins were its principal exponents. Homer was developing in his scenes of common life the power and breadth which made him the epic painter of America out-of-doors. Thomas Eakins, Philadelphia's stern realist, became the austere and powerful portraitist of the Reconstruction period in which stern advances in industrialism were colored by an often brutal calculation. Art, if considered at all, was regarded as little more than a stupid pastime. Eakins was a match for any of his sitters.

Contemporary with these men was a group who went to Europe not only for the superior training of the Continent but to breathe the air of artistic freedom, William Morris Hunt being one of the first Americans to study in France. Whistler, the brilliant, witty expatriate, and John La Farge were experimentalists and eclectics. Undergoing successively the influence of Courbet and of the English pre-Raphaelites, Whistler accepted Japanese ideas of formal composition and finally drew upon the dark impressionism of Velázquez. His full-length portrait of the critic *Théodore Duret* was characteristic of his fastidious and rather slender grace. La Farge, with more coherence, absorbed the tradition of Titian and Rubens and Delacroix. He was in a sense the American version of Ruskin and William Morris, experimenting in mosaic and painted glass, and at the same time expounding the gospel of humanism in contradiction to Whistler's doctrine of art for art's sake. While Whistler was becoming the idol of

WOODPECKERS–J. AUDUBON
(1785–1851)

LAKE GEORGE–KENSETT
(1818–1872)

AUTUMN OAKS–INNESS
(1825–1894)

FUR TRADERS ON MISSOURI–BINGHAM
(1811–1879)

THE AMERICAN SCHOOL

MME. X. – SARGENT
(1856–1925)

SELF-PORTRAIT
LA FARGE (1885–1910)

DURET – WHISTLER
(1834–1903)

TOILERS OF THE SEA – A. P. RYDER
(1847–1917)

MAX SCHMITT – EAKINS (1844–1916)

GULF STREAM – HOMER (1836–1910)

THE AMERICAN SCHOOL

HURRICANE, BAHAMAS—WINSLOW HOMER

BETWEEN ROUNDS—THOMAS EAKINS
Philadelphia Museum of Art

WOMAN AND CHILD DRIVING—MARY CASSATT
Philadelphia Museum of Art

TYROLESE CRUCIFIX—JOHN SINGER SARGENT

HEADED FOR BOSTON—MARIN
Private Collection (Artext Junior Print 425)

STRING QUARTETTE—J. LEVINE

WATER—C. SHEELER

SOUTH OF SCRANTON—P. BLUME

PONTE DELLA PAGLIA—M. PRENDERGAST
Washington. Phillips Memorial Gallery

Chelsea, John Singer Sargent, twenty years his junior, and destined to succeed him in popularity in the British capital, was studying with Carolus Durand in Paris and at the Louvre, where he, too, became fascinated by Velázquez and Frans Hals.

Mary Cassatt, the intimate friend and disciple of Degas, worked in Paris, while other artists went to Germany to study under the romantic masters at Munich and at Düsseldorf. They added their own contribution to the disciplines of the German studios, which operated on the basic principle that brushwork was the foundation of painting, a principle that soon became the byword of American academicians. At home, while Winslow Homer and Thomas Eakins were running the gamut of the American spirit in art, another side of the national temper was being portrayed in the sensitive mystical works of Albert Pinkham Ryder.

The Modern Movement established itself in America at the celebrated Armory Show in New York in 1913 when many of the European radicals were shown. Sponsored by "The Eight," including such men as Davies, Henri, Sloan, Luks, Glackens, and Prendergast, who had studied in Europe with the Impressionist masters, the movement was enthusiastically taken up. American painting, dominated by the School of Paris for a period of ten years after the First World War, has at last broken

LIGHTHOUSE AT TWO LIGHTS–EDWARD HOPPER
Private Collection (Artext Junior Print 376)

AMERICAN GOTHIC–GRANT WOOD
The Art Institute of Chicago (Artext Junior Print 877)

ROASTING EARS – BENTON

LOBSTER FISHERMEN – HARTLEY

TOM KENNEY COMES HOME – MECHAU

away and become a native expression of our time. In the work of Speicher, Bellows, Sheeler, Burchfield, Hopper, Demuth, Sterne and many others, we see a desire to find whatever is beautiful in the American scene and to paint it in clear simple terms. It is, however, against this national spirit in art that the abstract and experimental schools of the present day have so violently revolted. The future course of the American artist who, like the layman, is now at the crossroads in politics and economics, may not be clear for another generation.

DRAGON – W. BAZIOTES

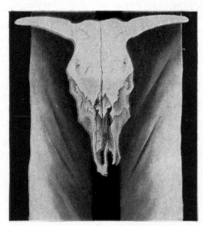

COW'S SKULL – O'KEEFFE

I SAW THE FIGURE 5 IN GOLD – DEMUTH

BEAUTIFICATION – WEBER